SUPERBLOOM

A Blessing for *Superbloom*

In Genesis 8:22 the Bible tells us as long as the earth endures, there will be seed time and harvest. Many things in the natural parallel with the supernatural. One of these examples is a natural occurrence that is called *superbloom.*

Seeds that have been sown come to life after years of being dormant. Even in Death Valley that reaches temperatures of 130 degrees you can experience a surprising manifestation of almost every kind and color of flower imaginable. If it happens in the natural, it will happen in the supernatural.

We have witnessed superbloom in our life, in our business, and our family. When you are faithful to God, He supplies everything you need. It has been a blessing to see what God has done through the leadership of Pastor Jeff Jenkins at Anchor Church. Every Sunday you can see that God is doing a sovereign work in His people. We recommend you read this book to better understand that God has sown more into you than you can imagine and He also never forgets the seed you sow.

A prayer:

God, I thank You that when I bring my tithes and offerings to the storehouse, You will open the windows of heaven over me and pour out a blessing so big that I will not be able to have room for all you do for me. You rebuke the devourer that would try to destroy me or my blessing, You fight for me. I am ready for the season of Superbloom.

Malachi 3:10–11

—**Judy and Paul Pogue**
Founders of Pogue Construction,
Pogue Family Missions, Minutemen Disaster Response.
Judy is also the Author of *Awaken Sleeping Beauty*.

Praise for *Superbloom*

Brennan Manning once lamented that many spiritual leaders are like travel agents passing out brochures to places they've never been. Neither Jeff Jenkins nor *Superbloom* is that. I've known Pastor Jeff more than 20 years now. He, his wife Sarah, and the community of believers they serve (Anchor Church), have lived and are living so much of the content within these pages.

I found *Superbloom* to be biblically-rich, thought-provoking, heart-piercing, and quite practical when it comes to cultivating a life in step with the Spirit of God and in the context of community with others. Take it in, walk it out, and watch God work.

—**Chris Seidman**
Lead Pastor, The Branch Church

Jeff Jenkins is a teaching pastor with a dynamic and exploding church in McKinney, Texas, and he is my friend. When he speaks you can hear his passion for King Jesus and the Kingdom, and when he writes, there is a depth of compassion for the reader that is compelling. What is a Superbloom, what does *pneumatikos* mean, and what does the relationship between seed, ground, and water have to do with my life?

The Study Guide at the conclusion of each chapter is a brilliant way to help us retain and internalize what is contained in each teaching. In fact, these pages could easily be used as a daily devotional to pray through some rough places in our past or present, in preparation for a glorious future.

When asked, "Why did you write this book?" Pastor Jeff says, "At the heart of it all [this book is about] a God who loves you enough to fill you with His Spirit, trust you with His power, and invite you into partnership with His purposes."

—Paul Wilbur
Renowned American Messianic Jewish worship leader,
singer-songwriter and author of *A King is Coming,*
Roar From Zion, and *Touching the Heart of God*

Jeff and Sarah have been friends and family in ministry for over 20 years. *Superbloom* is a thoughtful, Spirit-formed invitation into deeper understanding of how the Word and Spirit work in bringing about the heart of God through His people. Jeff honors Scripture while embracing the ongoing work of the Holy Spirit, offering a hopeful and grounded vision for the Church today. No matter what Christian tradition you come from, I believe you will find inspiration and invitation into the good life in Jesus within these pages.

—**Dusty Rush**
Teaching Pastor, Campus Church, Norcross, GA

Many believers sit in church as consumers instead of contributors—and Jeff refuses to let anyone stay comfortable there. He exposes the subtle lie that spiritual power belongs only to those on the platform and boldly reminds us all that so-called "ordinary" believers carry God-given, supernatural potential.

Superbloom doesn't read like a theology manual; it feels like a wake-up call. It's clear, practical, and filled with activating prayers and daily rhythms that move believers from inspiration to transformation. If you've ever felt overlooked, sidelined, or unsure where you fit, this book will shift your perspective—reminding you that your everyday life is sacred ground and that you were created to flourish right where you are, right now.

—**Shawn Brann**
Founder, GO&TELL | Ignite Europe

Superbloom is a beautiful picture of what happens to a life fully surrendered. Jeff didn't just write a book filled with information—it reads more like a roadmap to follow. He writes with vivid imagery, passion, and honesty. It's been one of the honors of my life to witness his testimony up close and to see him invite others into the supernatural power of the Holy Spirit. I know this book will be an incredible blessing to the body of Christ.

—**Michael Bethany**
International Speaker and Recording Artist

As someone without limbs who faces impossible circumstances daily, I have stood in the tension of needing a miracle healing myself and being used by God to bring miracles to others. I've never had hands or arms, but God still uses my heart to lay his hands on millions and activates many levels of healings. This deepens my love for the Spirit & God's love. *Superbloom* inspires believers to drink deep of the Holy Spirit and see the pure seed of God's Word & the fresh rain of God's Spirit bring dynamic harvest in His ways for His glory in His timing. My family is witnessing a beautiful Superbloom with Pastor Jeff in McKinney, Texas and around the world. Regardless of what you believe about the Spirit of God and His gifts, this book will expand your heart in ways that change everything, because our God truly has NO limits!

—**Nick Vujicic**
Evangelist & Author, Founder of NickV Ministries

I've known Jeff Jenkins for many years, and *Superbloom* feels like the distilled wisdom of a life faithfully walked with God. This book isn't about hype, platforms, or chasing the next spiritual experience—it's a deeply honest invitation back to sincerity, surrender, and the quiet power of the Holy Spirit at work in ordinary, faithful lives. What I especially appreciate is how Jeff gives clear, biblical language for both the gifts of the Spirit and the fruit of the Spirit, holding power and character together in a way that feels grounded, pastoral, and deeply needed right now. He writes as a pastor who has been through the desert and come out with humility, clarity, and hope, reminding us that what looks dormant is often just waiting on God's timing. *Superbloom* will challenge you, steady you, and ultimately draw you closer to the life God has already planted within you.

—**Michael Mistretta**
CEO of FIRM (Fellowship of Israel Related Ministries)
and Jerusalem Encounter

Do you want to grow? Really grow? Pastor Jeff Jenkins has the answer. Life is about seeds. They lead to life. You will quickly read and enjoy Jeff's mixture of stories, teaching and scripture to understand the secret. If you plant the right seeds (removing past bad ones), and spend time in prayer, the Word of God, and the Holy Spirit, your Superbloom is coming.

—Kelly Shackelford
President, CEO and Chief Counsel of
First Liberty Institute

Jeff has been my friend and co-laborer in ministry for more than thirty years. I've watched him grow from his football -playing days at LSU into the man of God he is today. The Lord has shaped him, stretched him, and entrusted him with gifts that continue to bless others. *Superbloom* reflects the man I know—sincere in faith, courageous in conviction, and deeply rooted in Christ. This book will challenge and inspire believers to trust God completely and step into the spiritual abundance He has prepared for them.

—Donnie Williams
Lead Pastor, Devoted City Church

SUPERBLOOM

*When All God's Gifts
in You Begin to Flourish*

JEFF JENKINS

Superbloom: When All God's Gifts in You Begin to Flourish

Copyright © 2026 by Jeff Jenkins

Unless otherwise noted, all Scripture quotations are taken from The Holy Bible, New International Version®, NIV®. Copyright © 1973, 1978, 1984, 2011 by Biblica, Inc. Used with permission of Zondervan. All rights reserved worldwide. www.zondervan.com

Scripture quotations marked (CEB) are taken from the COMMON ENGLISH BIBLE. © Copyright 2011 COMMON ENGLISH BIBLE. All rights reserved. Used by permission. (www.CommonEnglishBible.com)

Scripture quotations marked (ESV) are taken from the ESV® Bible (The Holy Bible, English Standard Version®), © 2001 by Crossway, a publishing ministry of Good News Publishers. Used by permission. All rights reserved. The ESV text may not be quoted in any publication made available to the public by a Creative Commons license. The ESV may not be translated in whole or in part into any other language. Used by permission. All rights reserved.

Scripture quotations marked (GNT) are from the Good News Translation in Today's English Version-Second Edition Copyright © 1992 by American Bible Society. Used by Permission.

Scripture quotations marked (ISV) are taken from the Holy Bible: International Standard Version©. Copyright © 1996-2012 by The ISV Foundation. ALL RIGHTS RESERVED INTERNATIONALLY. Used by permission.

Scripture quotations marked (NASB) are taken from the (NASB®) New American Standard Bible®, Copyright © 1960, 1971, 1977, 1995, 2020 by The Lockman Foundation. Used by permission. All rights reserved. www.Lockman.org

Scripture quotations marked (NKJV) taken from the New King James Version®. Copyright © 1982 by Thomas Nelson. Used by permission. All rights reserved.

Scripture quotations marked (NLT) are taken from the Holy Bible, New Living Translation, copyright ©1996, 2004, 2015 by Tyndale House Foundation. Used by permission of Tyndale House Publishers, Carol Stream, Illinois 60188. All rights reserved.

All rights reserved. No portion of this publication may be reproduced, stored in a retrieval system, or transmitted in any form by any means—electronic, mechanical, photocopying, recording, or any other—without prior permission from the publisher.

ISBN 979-8-9932552-4-8 paperback

ISBN 979-8-9932552-5-5 hardcover

ISBN 979-8-9932552-6-2 eBook

myanchorchurch.com

myanchorcollective.com

@myanchorchurch

Cover design and typeset by Peyton Sepeda, WildCreativePublishing.com

While the author makes every effort to provide accurate URLs at the time of printing for external or third-party internet websites, neither they nor the publisher assume any responsibility for changes or errors made after publication.

Printed in the United States of America

26 27 28 29 30—5 4 3 2 1

CONTENTS

FOREWORD

THE SPIRIT-EMPOWERED life is what we all seek after. We are trying to love Jesus more, pray more effectively, and minister to others with greater freedom.

Superbloom is Jeff Jenkins' journey toward a Spirit-filled life. It began in a cessationist background and ended up in a mighty river of the gifts of the Spirit.

Along the way, his journey was guided by the Scriptures and by what they teach us about being led by the Spirit.

My Dad, Roy Stockstill, had a similar story in 1963.

Dad was a Southern Baptist pastor who grew progressively hungrier for the Spirit's power. After reading the testimony of Dennis Bennett, an Episcopal rector at St. Mark's Episcopal Church in Van Nuys, California, his quest got serious.

He was the president of the Southern Baptist pastors conference in Baton Rouge (about 40 pastors). A fellow pastor came to his home one day and said he had been filled with the Spirit. My Dad (and later my mother) received a few short phrases of prayer in the Spirit.

Sixty-three years ago, that changed our world.

While Dad was sharing his experience with those forty pastors at their monthly meeting, one pastor asked, "What difference has this experience made in your daily life?"

He turned to the blackboard and wrote four letters: "REST." Putting down the chalk, he said to them, "Brethren, I used to work FOR God. Now, I work WITH God."

This book is a manual on how to work "with God." We know that the Spirit lives in you in a measure when we are born again. He comes to live in you when you are born again, "born of the Spirit." The fullness of the Spirit will be released out of you when your willing, surrendered spirit allows Him to manifest THROUGH you.

There are *"gifts, services, and activities"* (1 Corinthians 12:4, ESV). Paul did his best to help the Corinthian congregation release all of those manifestations without allowing the flesh to enter in and bring confusion.

My father's small utterance in the prayer language opened his life to "rivers of living water." He maintained his firm anchor in the inerrancy of Scripture while being open to the manifestations of the Book of Acts. He knew that any work of the Spirit would certainly result in the salvation of the lost and the spread of missions worldwide.

Bethany Church began in his living room that fall of 1963. Since that time, tens of thousands of people have been saved. Nine campuses have been established. In the 28 years I was pastoring the church, 63 million dollars were given to missions (local and foreign).

One pastor said to Dad after his testimony was given to those forty pastors, *"It will all blow over."* Dad liked to remind himself, *"It blew all over Baton Rouge, over the U.S., and all over the world!"*

Open yourself up to more.

Take the limits off the power of the Holy Spirit in your life. Guard yourself from excesses and anything that does not match the "ways of God" as well as the "acts of God."

I give glory to God for His healing power in my body, or I would not be able to write this foreword. We do not know everything about healing, but "see through a glass darkly." What we do know is that faith in the Gospels was always rewarded with God fulfilling His promises.

Superbloom means spiritual "water in the desert." It is giving your gifts the water they desperately need to activate your invisible potential.

I've been living that way for many, many years. Jeff and I want that for you so badly. If you are dry, parched, discouraged, weak, bound, or even broken, consider letting God open the "rock in the wilderness." There can only be one result from that miracle: *"much fruit."*

—Larry Stockstill
Pastors Emeritus, Bethany Church, Baton Rouge, La.
Founder of the Surge Project and Pastors University

JEFF JENKINS IS more than a gifted communicator or a pastor; he is a close personal friend and a brother in the truest sense of the word. Our lives became linked on a March afternoon in 2015 at a restaurant in McKinney, Texas. Jeff shared a prophetic dream he'd had years earlier—a dream that specifically mentioned my father, Larry Stockstill, and a vision to plant a million churches. That lunch wasn't just a meeting; it was a "holy ground" moment that changed the trajectory of both our lives.

As you read this, you aren't just getting information; you are holding the distilled wisdom of a man who has been through the fire. Jeff writes with a raw honesty that can only come from someone who has navigated deep seasons of brokenness and emerged with victory and hope. He mentions me throughout this book, but the text only scratches the surface of how we have personally walked together through some of the most trying times in both of our lives.

Jeff was there for me during the darkest hours of my father's terminal diagnosis. I remember sitting at a table with him on June 30, 2023, having to share the news that my father had only thirty days to live. In that moment of profound sorrow, Jeff didn't just offer empty words; he offered faith and a steady presence that anchored me. At the same time, I have stood by Jeff as he navigated the heavy pressures of leadership and the personal sacrifices required to lead Anchor Church. We have wept together, laughed a lot, eaten too much Cajun food, and reminded one another of God's promises when the "dry season" felt like it would never end.

Jeff's greatest strength is his refusal to settle for "performative faith." He has seen the lure of success and the hollowness of ministry hype, and he has decisively turned his back on it to pursue a sincere, authentic faith. He understands that the real work of the Spirit isn't about human willpower; it's about a "Total Gift Package" already deposited in you at salvation, waiting for the rain of the Spirit to hit it.

What I want you to know about Jeff is that the man you see in these chapters is the same man I know in private. He is a faithful steward who cares more about his walk with God than the size of his platform.

Superbloom is a roadmap for anyone who feels stuck in perpetual winter. It's a call to stop just "sipping religion" and start drinking deeply from the Spirit. I recommend this book, but more importantly, I recommend the man behind it. Read this with an expectant heart and get ready for things to start growing in your life that you thought were dead.

—**Joel E. Stockstill**
Surge, Executive Director

WHAT IS A SUPERBLOOM?

BOTANICAL PERSPECTIVE:

A superbloom is a rare desert botanical phenomenon in which an unusually high proportion of wildflowers, whose seeds have lain dormant in desert soil for years, germinate and bloom at roughly the same time.

Because of the heavy rains in late 2025 and even into January 2026, Death Valley, California, is expected to experience an exceptionally strong wildflower season in the spring of 2026, when this book is being published.

SPIRITUAL PERSPECTIVE:

A superbloom is a supernatural awakening of what is dormant in a person, a congregation, or even a region of people. It happens when the Holy Spirit activates the seeds of salvation, truth, calling, effort, gifts of grace, and even seeds of investment—causing personal growth, corporate vibrancy, ministry fruitfulness, and spiritual harvest to flourish visibly and powerfully.

The fact that we're in a botanical superbloom right now as this book is being published is amazing. In October 2024, we planned the 2025 entire year's sermon series at Anchor Church. I sensed the theme word for 2025 would be "Superbloom," and that there would be a supernatural flourishing in that year. This was related to a prophetic word from Larry Stockstill back in 2020 about Anchor in 2025. I preached a series called *Superbloom* in the summer of 2025, and then the rain came in the desert in late 2025—and the Superbloom is happening as this book is launching.

All I can say is, Lord, send the rain! We love You.

Best Ahead!

Jeff Jenkins standing in the actual Superbloom in Death Valley, March 3, 2026.
This was after the record rainfall in the later weeks of 2025.

WHEN THE DESERT BLOOMS

The seed is the word of God … But the seed on good soil stands for those with a noble and good heart, who hear the word, retain it, and by persevering produce a crop.

—Luke 8:11

Being filled with the Spirit is simply this - having my whole nature yielded to His power. When the whole soul is yielded to the Holy Spirit, God Himself will fill it.

—Andrew Murray

ON JULY 4, 2025, I wrote this introduction from a cabin in Whitefish, Montana. I was on my sabbatical, a time I take every five years to step away from the demands of ministry and dedicate space to rest, be refreshed, enjoy my family, and hear from God about the next season.

But this sabbatical felt profoundly different from the one five years before. In June 2020, I sat on this same mountain, spiritually, emotionally, and physically depleted. I was addicted to approval, terrified of rejection, embarrassed by imperfections, and ashamed of all that was leading to failure. I had a lot of great definitions and explanations for things in the faith but I lacked very much valuable substance for what I was experiencing.

The world was locked down. Anchor Church had been forced online. We were four years old as a church, and attendance on our best day was about 1,800 people. But now, we weren't meeting at all. The staff was fractured. Our young eldership was divided, even more so than I realized. Even before the pandemic, I knew there were some cracks in the foundation, and once the shutdown hit, those cracks became craters. Nothing remained hidden. It was like rain hitting dry ground. Everything buried in the soil began to manifest, and much of it was unhealthy.

I knew much of the fault was mine. I was the leader. But I couldn't admit it, at least not yet. I was scared, and I was angry. Angry at myself, friends, lies, rumors, the government, the media, riots, fires, protests, and everything else. My soul was in the worst place it had ever been.

Everything I feared most about ministry collapse was happening.

Fast.

And worse than I knew at the time.

I couldn't breathe spiritually, so I flew to Montana on June 1, 2020. After I landed in Kalispell, my phone buzzed. It was Andrew Gwynn, my closest friend. He and his wife, Celeste, are the people you dream of planting a church with. Andrew's message was short: "Hey Jeff, I don't expect you to respond to this. Celeste's mom just passed. I knew you'd want to know."

Now I wanted to fly back home. How could I miss Linda Nevil's funeral? Because everything was locked down, her family had not been allowed to see her for the final weeks of her life. Linda died alone in her assisted living home. Why? COVID-19 and all the rules that isolated people in such a chaotic time.

I had a Skype call with my therapist, and after the session ended, I was broken. I begged God, "Tell me what to do, and I'll do it." He responded, "Buy a one-man tent, water, and wood. Go to the place I'll show you. Fast. Be with Me alone the rest of your time here."

I had fourteen days left, so I went to the store and bought what I needed. I ended up twenty miles off the highway at Hungry Horse

Reservoir, near Glacier National Park. For the next two weeks, I ate no food and drank only water. I read several books on my Kindle app. I journaled extensively. I kept the same fire burning the entire time. And most importantly, God broke through.

THE DESERT

That 2020 sabbatical shook everything I thought I knew about the Lord, faith, prayer, miracles, ministry, and especially myself. I thought I understood ministry in the Spirit, but I couldn't even breathe. I could still speak and explain the things of the Spirit but I cringed at even the best words of faith from my own mouth. I was dangerously numb to joy; yet, fully tormented with pain.

I spent those fourteen days fasting and asking God if there was anything left in the ground of my life worth cultivating. I was depressed. I was so dry. I was barren. I questioned my calling, my competence, and much more than that. It felt like everything God had planted in me over decades was buried under disappointment, embarrassment, shame, and exhaustion. I asked Him a hundred times, "Is there anything else in the ground, Lord?"

There was almost nothing in me that could keep going except a few seeds of hope. Some people had told me, "If it all falls apart, and it's just us, we'd do it again with you." I don't even know if they meant it, but their words stayed planted in the soil of my heart.

That's when the Lord began to show me that what I thought was death was actually dormancy. What I saw as an ending was really a season of hidden preparation. God wasn't asking me to start over. He was asking me to surrender, to let Him awaken what had always been there.

Because here's the truth I had missed for so long: If you cannot enjoy the rich pleasures of true peace, then you will be enslaved to selfish desires in every facet of life. You'll see that the Spirit's work in our lives usually becomes known the closer we get to a simple freedom from broken passions, desires, and ambition.

The Holy Spirit's most powerful work begins the moment we believe. Believing doesn't usually happen in fullness of power until selfish ambition, survival, pride, and fear of man prove to be painfully empty.

Every believer receives what Paul calls "the manifestation of the Spirit for the common good" (1 Corinthians 12:7 ESV). Not some believers. Not special or uniquely called believers. *Every believer.* This comes with full access at salvation and experienced in greater measures as you mature.

Unfortunately, every greater measure of fullness also comes with some imperfection mixed with it, and even our most precious learning comes with a shadow of some form of darkness eventually. You'll wonder if you're missing something quite often. You'll wonder if you are doing it all right and if there's more.

You have to know this, there is no "Christian starter pack" with optional upgrades. From day one, you receive the full spiritual toolkit deposited by the Holy Spirit, activated by faith, and developed through maturity. Through steady ongoing faith and surrender, you will carry the actual power of God forward and impact your world with humility, knowing it's Him working His love through you.

SUPERBLOOM

Only a couple months before the shutdown, Larry Stockstill (one of my heroes in the faith) stood with me on the land Anchor Church had just purchased. He prophesied: "It's going to get very difficult. You won't see a way forward. But God will provide. Before year five, there will be a superbloom." Larry said a lot more, but that's what I remember most.

As things dried up and went dormant, I hated the thought of waiting on rain for some "superbloom" I didn't understand. But let me tell you: A superbloom from the Lord is worth the wait. If I only knew then what I know now.

Our church didn't just survive; God gave us new birth. In many ways, we're not the same. These last five years have taught me three truths I wish I had known decades ago.

1. A Superbloom Reveals What's in You.

Here's what I know: you didn't create the laws of the soil of your life. God did. Just as He governs the laws of harvest on the earth, He shaped your spiritual soil. Every spiritual gift, calling, and scar has been shaped by a sovereign God who sees the end from the beginning. He cultivates with purpose, and even the wilderness seasons are part of His preparation.

Your past does not disqualify you from supernatural fruitfulness. And even though you feel there's too much sin in the soil of your heart for God to do anything good, the seeds of faith are still there. The seeds are the Spirit who filled you the moment you believed, the gifts given to you at salvation, the Word planted in you through Scripture and truth. You are not too old, too young, too broken, or too ordinary. You are a field prepared by the Master Gardener, and He knows exactly what He planted and when it's meant to bloom.

2. A Superbloom Reveals Your Stewardship.

One day, I received a supernatural, God-appointed voicemail: "Pastor Jeff, this is Brad. Call me back. Tyree and I have something we need to tell you." Brad and Tyree are wonderful people we served with in Florida, and as kingdom-minded business leaders, they had made a large contribution to Anchor Church. I didn't want to call Brad now, though, because he'd probably heard how things were falling apart.

Still, something made me pick up the phone and dial his number. Brad said, "Hey, Tyree and I were sitting on our back porch listening to your sermon, and we both heard the Holy Spirit say, *Call Pastor Jeff and see if he needs help.* We don't know what that means, but we feel like He's telling us to move to McKinney and come help you."

Only God knew how much Brad and Tyree's obedience would shape the next four years. They jumped in and helped rebuild Anchor's staff, infrastructure, and ministries. And they even continued to invest financially. Their partnership taught me that a superbloom is not a random or wished-for blessing; it is the reward of consistent, daily stewardship.

Many believers expect the bloom without the farming, but spiritual gifts grow through activation. Character matures through obedience. God knows who He can trust with increase, and ministry fruit multiplies through faithfulness.

3. A Superbloom Multiplies Through What You Sow.

The ultimate purpose of a superbloom isn't your own fulfillment but the multiplication of fruit in others. At Anchor Church, our burden is to bring hope to people everywhere. We call this vision "The Front

Porch Life," and it's our roadmap for stewarding everything God has given us for His glory.

You have your own assignment. As you live, serve, and give, what's inside you begins to transform what's around you. God planted seeds in you for His glory and His mission. You may never see the full harvest in your lifetime, but the seeds you sow now will continue to bear fruit for generations.

———

Before we go any further, I need to give you both a warning and a promise.

Warning

This journey will disrupt your comfort. If you come from a background that is skeptical of spiritual gifts or wary about spiritual manipulation, I get it. I really do. And if you've tried to operate in these gifts but felt like you were missing something, you're not alone.

A superbloom requires involvement, hunger, risk, surrender, and growth. You can't pursue the authentic gifts of the Spirit and remain spiritually passive. You can't stay anonymous, hidden in the back row, and unaffected. You'll face resistance from religious systems, skeptical friends, insecure leaders, and even your own fear. You'll wrestle with doubts. You'll make mistakes as you learn to discern and steward supernatural power. And you'll make mistakes, do spiritual things with flawed motives and you will certainly be misunderstood by someone.

If you walk this road with sincere faith and a tender heart, if you'll repent of any fear of man, forget every hindrance you have to the Holy Spirit—you won't have to check your mind at the door. Go all in with your whole being.

Wherever you are in your experience, if you turn to Him, He will meet you right where you are and show you who He is. You'll flourish in His love, His wisdom, the pure revelation of what He has for you; fresh power and the fruits of the Spirit.

A superbloom isn't about becoming more charismatic. Yes, we're going to explore the gifts of the Spirit, but even more so, this is an invitation to the life you were created for. I believe you'll experience great joy in experiencing all that God deposited in the soil of your heart.

I believe gifts that have been buried for years or even decades are about to burst into bloom. Ordinary people are going to walk in extraordinary power. And the Church is about to become more radiant than we've seen in centuries.

The Lord who turned water into wine, fed thousands with a boy's lunch, and walked out of the grave is still moving, and He wants to move through *you*.

The seeds are planted.

The rain is falling.

Welcome to the superbloom.

For from him and through him and to him are all things. To him be glory forever. Amen.

—Romans 11:36 ESV

TO GET THE MOST FROM THIS BOOK

- **Read with an open Bible.** Every chapter is saturated with Scripture. Look up the passages and let God's Word guide you.

- **Read with an open heart.** Ask the Holy Spirit to activate what He's placed in you. Be willing to have your assumptions challenged and your expectations stretched.

- **Read with a humble mind.** No matter your background, stay curious. Truth doesn't fear questions. The more humble you are, the more wise and at peace you'll be in all things.

- **Read in community.** This isn't just for individual growth. Form a small group, use the discussion questions, and pray together. Gifts grow best in family.

- **Read with expectation.** God wants this more than you do. He's waiting for you to believe what He's already given.

- **Read with patience.** Noticeable growth rarely happens overnight. Some seeds sprout quickly while others take seasons. Don't compare timelines. Stay faithful.

You may never see the full harvest, but the seeds you sow will bear fruit for generations.

1

AWAKEN WHAT'S DORMANT

Our theology and experience of the Spirit must be more interwoven if our experienced life of the Spirit is to be more effective.

—**Gordon D. Fee,** *Paul, the Spirit, and the People of God*

For this reason I remind you to fan into flame the gift of God,
which is in you.

—**2 Timothy 1:6**

I GREW UP deeply involved the White's Ferry Road Church of Christ in West Monroe, Louisiana. Faith wasn't flashy or performed. It was lived. Every Sunday, from 1973 until I graduated from high school in 1992, gospel-centered truth formed the foundation of my soul. Before *Duck Dynasty* ever made them famous, the Robertsons were my friends, mentors, and fellow leaders. Willie, Jase, Missy, Korie, and I were all part of the church's student ministry leadership. Every Sunday night, dozens of us packed into Korie's parents' home to worship, study Scripture, and lead our friends to Christ.

Nobody had to hype it.

Nobody had to bribe kids to come. Sincere faith was forged through discipleship and relationships, not programs. Spiritual growth happened through surrender, not strategies.

My closest friends were young believers who actually *believed*. We were discipled one-on-one. We shared the gospel face-to-face with our friends and baptized dozens of them day or night wherever there was water, just like they did in the book of Acts. We memorized

Scripture because we wanted to know God and effectively witness, not impress anyone.

Looking back, I realize how rare that was. We weren't chasing platforms. We were just trying to follow Jesus and make a difference. And it stuck.

Fast forward to 2000.

I became a full-time lead pastor, and God began blessing the ministry with growth. In 2003, I became the senior pastor of a wonderful congregation in East Texas. During that time, my friend Dusty Rush invited me to join him with a group of young preachers; Chris Seidman and Tim Spivey, among others. We were all in our early thirties and were all in over our heads a bit. We craved mentoring and guidance from some of our heroes, like Rick Atchley, Max Lucado, Randy Harris, and others. These moments were pure and full of life for me. I still value those men and honor their integrity and love for the word and service.

Things began to change quickly. We grew significantly. Somewhere in the momentum, I found something I wasn't prepared for: the seductive pull of numerical success. What started as pure gospel impact began competing with church growth strategies, branding sessions, target-market-focused sermon series, and the pressure to keep outperforming last Sunday. I was measuring fruit with the wrong ruler, and it started to mess with the foundation I'd received in West Monroe.

Then came 2006.

After a forty-day fast, I had an encounter with the Holy Spirit that helped me understand Him more fully. Within weeks, I was operating in gifts I thought had ceased, discerning God's voice in prayer and Scripture and through others speaking. I was always suspicious of people who said, "God spoke to me." But I started to experience what they were talking about. I knew His voice more clearly than ever, and I was walking into moments I couldn't explain other than *This is the Holy Spirit.*

I could no longer hold to the *cessationist* belief that the miraculous gifts like prophecy, healing, tongues, and miracles ceased with the deaths of the apostles and the completion of the biblical canon. I had so much to learn about how to even understand what I was experiencing.

There are also those whom I'd call *practical Cessationists*, who may not be *theologically opposed to* the gifts but have never experienced them in a meaningful way. They live as if the Spirit no longer moves in that manner, not because they doubt God's power but because they're cautious (and reasonably so).

I entered a whole new world of ministry as a *Continuationist.* I believe that all the gifts of the Spirit "continue" or are still active and available today through the Spirit's power. I began ministering alongside leaders of some of the largest charismatic churches in America. I traveled to forty-three nations, helping train and encourage leaders and thousands of pastors from nearly every denomination.

I've witnessed revivals with hundreds of thousands of people in attendance that changed entire geographical territories. I've seen raw hunger for Jesus. On the other hand, I've also seen embarrassing hype. I've seen church splits that destroyed families. I've been in both greenrooms with celebrity pastors and mud huts with unknown heroes. From cessationist scholarship to charismatic excess, from megachurch stages to remote villages, I've walked through it all. And I've come to this conclusion: We don't need better strategies for growth. We need real rain on real seed. We need the real Spirit to awaken the real people.

This book isn't about getting more of God as you grow. You already have full access to Him. It's about God getting more of you. He isn't looking for theological trophies or spiritual acrobats. He's looking for sincere faith, the kind He can fan into flame. What does that look like? It looks like your whole mind, will, and emotions being surrendered to the fullness of the Spirit of God who already lives in you.

The body of Christ is sitting on more spiritual potential than we can imagine. The gifts are there. The calling is there. The power is there. What's missing isn't another emotional experience. What's missing is the Word and Spirit being activated.

In other words, a superbloom.

We don't need better strategies for growth. We need real rain on real seed.

WHAT A SUPERBLOOM IS NOT

Let me be absolutely clear: A *superbloom* is not about awakening your inner potential, stirring your emotional energy, or discovering the divine spark of your soul. That's the language of self-help spirituality, Eastern mysticism, or modern humanism. This is different.

What lies dormant in you is not fleshly potential but the presence and power of the Holy Spirit. You don't need to awaken human willpower, personality, charm, or flow. I'm talking about what God has already poured out on you and deposited in you. This comes from above, through the Word, the Spirit, and the work of grace in your life.

When I speak of "activation," I'm talking about surrender. I'm talking about yielding to the Holy Spirit bringing what God already put in you and what He desires for you into full bloom. This happens only by yielded obedience.

This is not New Age mysticism or sensational hype. This is biblical discipleship with Spirit-empowered fruitfulness.

WHAT A SUPERBLOOM IS

There's a phenomenon that happens in Death Valley, California. For most of the year, that place looks exactly like its name suggests: *dead*. The ground cracks like a pale sea of peanut butter wafers, stretched and barren under the relentless sun. Tourists drive through and see nothing but emptiness, convinced that life has abandoned this forsaken place.

But they're wrong.

Death Valley isn't dead; it's dormant.

Hidden in those cracked surfaces are millions of seeds. They've been there for years, just waiting for the right conditions. Then, maybe once every decade, the heavens open up. Torrential rains flood the valley floor, and something miraculous happens. Within thirty days, that same barren landscape explodes into a carpet of wildflowers stretching as far as the eye can see. The same hopeless-looking soil transforms into one of the most breathtaking displays of life on earth.

They call it a "superbloom," and God wants to do the same thing in His Church, in her leaders, and in your life. Right now, there are seeds in the soil of our hearts. These seeds are the living Word of God, callings, giftings, dreams, prayers your grandmother prayed over you, encouragement from that teacher who believed in you, moments when God whispered your name, and so on.

Maybe you think those seeds are dead because you haven't seen them flourish. But I'm here to tell you they're dormant. They're just waiting for the Holy Spirit to pour out like rain and awaken everything God has deposited in you.

Soaked but Seedless

Have you ever tried to grow something in a pot of saturated soil with no seeds? No matter how much water you pour, nothing will grow. There may be emotion, spiritual hunger, and even openness to the supernatural. But without the Word of God, which is the seed, there's nothing for the Spirit to activate.

Word-Rich but Rain-Starved

On the other side, you can have soil packed with seed but entirely empty of moisture. The seed may be powerful and even loaded with life, but it's not going anywhere without water. A person can be full of knowledge, doctrine, and maybe even truth but still lack the personal presence and power of the Holy Spirit to make it come alive.

Where Word and Spirit Almost Seem Alike

This tension is both metaphorical and biblical. Throughout Scripture, the Word of God and the Spirit of God are described in ways that sometimes seem interchangeable. Here are just a few examples:

The Spirit gives life; the flesh counts for nothing. The words I have spoken to you—they are full of the Spirit and life. (John 6:63)

Take the sword of the Spirit, which is the word of God. (Ephesians 6:17 NLT)

For the word of God is alive and active.… it judges the thoughts and attitudes of the heart. (Hebrews 4:12 NLT)

All Scripture is God-breathed. (2 Timothy 3:16)

So is my word that goes out from my mouth: It will not return to me empty. (Isaiah 55:11)

Our gospel came to you not simply with words but also with power, with the Holy Spirit and deep conviction. (1 Thessalonians 1:5)

Prophets, though human, spoke from God as they were carried along by the Holy Spirit. (2 Peter 1:21)

Many theologians argue that the Spirit *is* the Word, meaning the only voice of the Spirit we need or should expect today is the written Word of God. While I agree that the Spirit will never contradict Scripture, I don't believe these verses mean He has stopped speaking.

A practical cessationist may say, "This morning in prayer, the Lord laid this Scripture on my heart, and I wanted to share it with you."

A Charismatic or Continuationist may say, "This morning in prayer, the Holy Spirit spoke to me, and I wanted to encourage you with what He said."

What's the difference?

There isn't one.

In both situations, the Holy Spirit speaks and makes His Word living and active.

I believe the Spirit illuminates, applies, activates, and personalizes the written Word. I also believe He speaks directly to the hearts of believers, always in alignment with the truth of Scripture but often with fresh conviction or prophetic clarity.

But What If the Seed Was Never Sown?

There's a practical tension that's been bothering me. I believe that every follower of Jesus already has the "total gift package," meaning the Spirit of God comes with everything you need for a full life of supernatural faith. We'll go over this more in depth in Chapter 3, but for now, suffice it to say that the Word-seed is there.

But what if it wasn't?

You can't manifest what isn't in you, and you can't harvest what hasn't been planted. Yes, someone can be filled with the Spirit, but the Spirit doesn't override ignorance. He activates what's been sown.

Jesus is the Word made flesh. His way, His truth, and His voice must be received by faith. The Spirit doesn't implant the Word by osmosis. The Word gets into the soil of your heart through hearing, reading, receiving, and responding.

In Romans 10:17, the apostle Paul writes, "Faith *comes* from hearing, and hearing by the word of Christ" (NASB). I often say, "Faith comes by *hearing* and *hearing* and *hearing* and *hearing* and *hearing*." Notice the active, present tense. *Hearing* is living, continuous exposure to God's Word. If it was a one-time encounter or static state, Paul would have written "having heard."

In short, the Spirit empowers what the Word reveals, and the Word forms what the Spirit fills. Without both, something essential is missing. If you're feeling dry in your faith, you might be *Word-rich but rain-starved*. You need the Holy Spirit to breathe fresh life into what you already know. Or if you're excited about spiritual gifts but feel unstable or shallow, taken advantage of, or continually let down by God, you might be *soaked but seedless*. You need to plant yourself in the truth of God's Word so the Spirit has something to bring to life.

Either way, you're not far from a bloom. When Spirit and Word come together and water meets seed, growth is inevitable.

Word-Rich but Rain-Starved	vs.	Soaked but Seedless
Biblically grounded but spiritually dry		Spiritually sensitive but theologically shallow
Knows truth but lacks power		Feels power but lacks truth
Strong in doctrine, weak in encounter		Strong in emotion, weak in direction
May resist spiritual gifts		May resist spiritual discipline
Seed is present, but water is missing		Water is present, but seed is missing
Needs fresh filling of the Spirit		Needs grounding in the Word

THE SEDUCTION I DIDN'T SEE COMING

By 2003, I was invited into tight mentoring circles with men I deeply respected. I learned from the most successful church growth experts, revivalists, and ministry multipliers of my era:

- Rick Warren's *Purpose Driven Church* (I played his tapes until they warped).

- John Maxwell's leadership content (I devoured everything he wrote).

- Bill Hybels' Willow Creek Leadership Summits (I sat in the front row for the first four events in Chicago).

- Reinhard Bonnke's crusade systems (I studied them after my Holy Spirit encounter).

- Yonggi Cho's 720,000-member church model (I immersed myself in his lifestyle of discipleship and prayer).

It felt like college recruiting all over again. I was convinced that leadership is what everything rises and falls on and that to be our best, we had to adopt the best of the world's systems and strategies for growth. After all, we couldn't let the world be more successful than the church, right?

I became an expert in these world-class strategies, and yes, they certainly produced tremendous results. But when your ministry becomes your identity, you're not far from distraction or compromise.

How $5,000 Shoes Opened My Eyes

In 2014, I sat in an upscale restaurant with the pastoral team from one of America's largest churches, hosting a guest speaker whose name you'd recognize instantly. This dynamic pastor had just delivered a powerful sermon to thousands of students. His message was well-crafted, humorous, and moving. People responded to Christ during the altar call.

But over lunch, he asked a question that still stirs me in a bad way: "Okay, it's your last sermon you ever preach ... [intentional pause] What shoes are you wearing?"

I was expecting something like, "What text are you preaching?" or "Who do you want it to be with?" or "What's the burden you just have to get out?" The last thing on my mind was what shoes I'd want to be wearing.

The pastors at the table erupted in laughter and eagerly discussed:

- Their favorite brands

- The most impressive they'd seen or worn

- The psychology of footwear in communication

- How image impacts influence

- Whether Italian leather better communicated authenticity to different demographics.

For twenty long minutes, I felt old and out of touch. These weren't evil people. They were gifted, sincere leaders, but they were also shaping the ministry culture to agree that style mattered at least as much as substance, that image complemented anointing, and that the messenger overshadowed the message.

That moment crystallized something I'd been sensing but couldn't articulate: We've created a sophisticated substitute for the supernatural that's so convincing, we don't realize what we're missing. I've watched pastors succeed in ministry systems and live more lavishly than professional athletes, all justified by "maximizing their platform for kingdom impact."

I also realized this was the reason why I was buying certain shoes and trying to dress in certain ways. My disgust wasn't as much about the other pastors at the table, but about the realization of how I'd been influenced. I didn't like it.

The Intoxication of Growth

Let me be forthright about something most pastors will agree with: Church growth is intoxicating, and a lack of growth is also intoxicating. During my time as Executive Senior Pastor at a 15,000-member church, I watched guest speakers receive six-figure honorariums for weekend services. Brilliant leaders discussed market research more than prayer, and demographic analysis often trumped spiritual discernment.

I contributed to this problem because I simply didn't know any better then. No one taught me to be this way. It just came with the adrenaline-high growth atmospheres many of us flocked to and were drunkenly running in. The pressure to succeed, mixed with the lure toward comfort, security, and influence, slowly outweighed the desire for true devotion to Christ. I took the attractional church growth bait, and I drank the growth Kool-Aid. This intoxication spread beyond my heart to my ambition, my strategic default, and my consulting practices.

My focus in this book is not to shame what we've all done wrong in the past and explain how to do everything right going forward. I'm just getting back to the pure roots God gave me. I am returning to the core foundations of simple devotion and sincere expectations aligned with the Word of God. As I do this, I'm experiencing more hope, more vibrant joy, and much more meaningful contentment in what the Lord has for me in my one life.

The Spirit empowers what the Word reveals, and the Word forms what the Spirit fills.

3 TYPES OF SUPERBLOOM

When we get back to the true and pure seed of the Word of God, we begin to witness the natural results of abiding in His love and partnering with Him to change His world. Let me share how this works in my life today by unpacking the three types of superbloom. This foundation is essential for sustaining a Spirit-activated life over the long haul.

Personal Superbloom

Revival doesn't start around me. It starts within me. When I turn down the noise, tune in to the Spirit, and let the Word of God speak louder than my ambition or insecurity, something comes alive again. It's not hype. It's pure. It's holy. It's Him.

I'm getting back to my roots and experiencing more joy, power, and vibrancy today than I did when I first fell in love with Jesus. He's so good, and I want to bring Him more of my heart for all of my days.

This isn't about "being more Spirit-filled." If you've been born again, you've already received the gift of the Holy Spirit (Acts 2:38). He deposits Himself in you. He is powerful, personal, and fruitful in every believer and gives us immediate access to Himself. But what some call "the baptism of the Spirit" or "the Second Blessing" is really *activation*; when the Holy Spirit activates His gifts, power, and work into your soul and body and then through you in His ministry.

Your personal superbloom begins when what God planted finally starts showing up in how you live, love, and worship. Here are five Scriptures that show Jesus' desire for what He's planted in you to come alive, manifest, and bear lasting fruit in your personal experience:

This is to my Father's glory, that you bear much fruit, showing yourselves to be my disciples. (John 15:8)

But the fruit of the Spirit is love, joy, peace, forbearance, kindness, goodness, faithfulness, gentleness and self-control. (Galatians 5:22–23)

Whoever believes in me, as Scripture has said, rivers of living water will flow from within them. (John 7:38)

May the God of hope fill you with all joy and peace as you trust in him, so that you may overflow with hope by the power of the Holy Spirit. (Romans 15:13)

Now to him who is able to do immeasurably more than all we ask or imagine, according to his power that is at work within us. (Ephesians 3:20)

This is your superbloom promise: There is power already at work within you. It's not waiting to be imported from a conference. It's waiting to be activated from the Holy Spirit in and through your whole being.

How to Experience a Personal Superbloom Every Day

1. SEEK THE LORD

When you cease to seek comfort in anything created you will begin to truly seek the Lord. You'll find Him. To seek Him is to find Him. To reach for Him alone is to reach Him. He always closes the gap. You will be content in Him no matter what happens around you or to you. When you are zealous and diligent in seeking Him you will be made ready for all things. Peace will blow your mind with understanding.

No desire in life compares to seeking the Lord and delighting in Him alone—for His glory and nothing else.

2. TURN DOWN THE VOLUME

We live in a loud world, both inside and out. If you want the Spirit to activate what's inside you, start by creating rhythms of quiet throughout your day. I have these moments programmed in my phone before meetings, before I start work, when I finish work, before I go to a meal, and even before I enter my house. Before you scroll, post, or respond to anything, pause. Breathe. Say, "Holy Spirit, I'm here." That's how you begin to tune in again. The seed doesn't need hype; it needs stillness.

3. SURRENDER SOMETHING REAL

Nothing activates the manifestation of the Spirit more than intentionally surrendering something meaningful with the intent of drinking of the Spirit. Don't wait for a worship song to create the moment. Create it yourself. Each day, surrender something real. It could be your anxiety, your ambition, your agenda, and so on. A personal superbloom is a revival within, and you grow by handing over what's holding you back. Let go of what's on the surface so something deeper can rise.

4. REOPEN THE WORD WITH EXPECTANCY

When you read the Bible, delight in Him. It's where His Word and Spirit become living and active. Read it out loud and let your ears hear your mouth declaring the Word of God. This is when expectancy is created. You have to command your mind, will, and emotions to come into alignment with His Word.

The living Word brings spiritual encounters, so open your Bible like the soil opens to rain. Ask the Holy Spirit to highlight one truth and let it soak into you. One verse. One line. One promise that reclaims ground in your heart.

A personal superbloom starts with fresh revelation of the living Word coming alive again. You desperately need the Word of God in your soul. Read it. Hear it. Memorize it. Hide it. Confess it. Stand on it. Run in it.

5. RESPOND WITH WORSHIP

Nothing causes a man to rise up in worship more powerfully than simplicity and purity. Worship is very simple and increasingly pure. Worship is sincere devotion. Worship is more than listening to a song. It's a simple response and a pure posture. Every time the Spirit stirs something in you, whether peace, conviction, joy, longing, or something else, don't rush to post it. Don't publicly pretend that it's your mantra. And don't you dare brush it off.

Instead, speak it. Sing it. Kneel if you can. Go for a walk and pray out loud. Do whatever you have to do to keep your heart tender, simple and pure.

When gratitude rises, give it language.

When awe shows up, give it a voice.

When the Holy Spirit brings something to life inside you, avoid killing the moment by posting it or talking to others about it. Keep this pure.

6. EXPECT FRUIT, NOT FIREWORKS

Fireworks shoot up, dazzle, and fizzle out quickly. Fruit takes time to grow. Avoid those "get-rich-quick" ideas. Run from everything that avoids perseverance, long-suffering, patience, and hope. Look for fruit.

A personal superbloom might not feel dramatic. It might show up as unexpected peace in the middle of chaos or joy when nothing around you has changed. Both are supernatural. Don't wait for goosebumps, promotions, or more money to believe God is working and moving.

The Spirit's first work is transformation, not sensation. If you're becoming more loving, more patient, or more rooted in hope, then stay tenderhearted.

Praise Him.

You're blooming, and the fruit is real.

Corporate Superbloom

I intentionally spent time on the personal superbloom because that's where everything starts. But activation was never meant to remain personal. A **corporate superbloom** happens when what's alive in you and in others begins to come *together*. Some people call this a "corporate anointing." I call it what happens when surrendered people bring their hunger into the room and heaven responds.

Have you ever walked into a worship gathering and just *knew* something was different, like something *more* was in the atmosphere? Something weighty, alive, holy? That doesn't usually "just happen." It's not the set list. It's not the lighting. It's not the size of the room or the polish of the service. When a corporate superbloom breaks out, it's because something *in the people* begins to overflow, and God, in His mercy, *is experienced in the room.*

I've seen it happen again and again. Every weekend at Anchor Church, we host several live services. They're mostly full, and some are packed with overflow rooms, standing crowds, and buzzing in the hallways. Yes, there's usually more natural energy in the most crowded services, but that's not what I'm talking about. I'm not talking about hype or adrenaline-based energy. I'm talking about the manifest presence of the Holy Spirit.

Sometimes in the busiest services, there's a time crunch. The crowd is physically present but spiritually miles away. The worship seems great, but the altar remains empty. The gospel lands strong, but the response feels rushed. There's energy but weak momentum in the room.

But other times, even in a lightly filled gathering, I've sensed the Holy Spirit start to move like rain. Even if only 20 or 30 percent of the room came hungry, *that hunger becomes contagious.* And worship becomes simple, sincere, and pure. Hearts are tender. The Word flows with power. The room becomes sacred space.

That's not just a good Sunday. That's a corporate superbloom. It requires just a few people who are fully surrendered and deeply hungry. They walk in, not with the attitude of *What am I getting out of this?* but the expectation, *God, whatever You want to do in this room, I want to be part of it.*

A corporate superbloom happens when individual hunger becomes a collective atmosphere, and the presence of God moves not just *in* people but *among* them too. We see this all over Scripture.

- **Acts 2**: The believers devoted themselves to the apostles' teaching, to breaking bread, to prayer. The results were awe, unity, power, and favor.

- **Acts 4**: After the believers prayed, *"the place where they were meeting was shaken"* (v. 31).

- **1 Corinthians 14**: Paul writes that when unbelievers walk into a Spirit-filled gathering, they will fall under conviction and cry out, *"God is really among you!"* (v. 25).

This is what happens when we gather not just to consume but to *contribute* from what God is doing in each of us.

Have you ever been in a room where the worship was *more* than music? *Ministry to God* is not on the worship team. It's not on the preacher. It's not on the greeters or the sound systems or the lights. It's on *you.* It's on *me.*

What God is doing in you might be the rain someone else's seed is waiting on. The power of a corporate superbloom is that your personal surrender can become someone else's spiritual breakthrough.

How to Corporately Activate What You've Personally Cultivated

How do we cultivate this? How do we prepare for God to move in power, not just individually but together too?

1. PREPARE BEFORE YOU ARRIVE

My wife, Sarah, and I know how challenging it is to prepare for corporate worship. From 2008 until 2012, we drove over one hundred miles round trip multiple times per week for worship services with five kids under twelve. We know how distracting it is to get things ready, get to the building, get kids checked in, find seats, and dive in. But, we did it every week and never missed. This wasn't because we were pastors. At that time, we were non-staff church members like many of you.

We came in fully prepared, full of praise, worship, expectation, hunger, and an attitude to affect the area around us. It was an overflow of our life and devotion.

You never have to wait for the room to wake you up. Wake up the room by arriving already engaged. Pray for your church the day before. Pray for your pastor, the team, and the person who will sit next to you. Walk in ready. Change the room with faith & joy.

2. RESPOND PROMPTLY AND AUTHENTICALLY

When it's time to worship, *worship*. When it's time to pray, *pray*. When it's time to listen, *listen*. This sounds too simple, but your yes carries weight. Your obedience is part of the atmosphere God wants to fill.

3. RELEASE WHAT GOD HIGHLIGHTS

The Holy Spirit doesn't highlight things in you so you can keep them hidden. Maybe it's a word of encouragement. Maybe it's helping someone during ministry time. Maybe it's choosing to stay after service and genuinely see people. Whatever *it* is, act on the nudge. The corporate move of God you're longing for begins with surrendered saints. What if it's already sitting inside you, just waiting to be released?

Kingdom Superbloom

If the personal superbloom is what God awakens in you and the corporate superbloom is what God manifests among us when we gather, then the kingdom superbloom is what overflows through us into the world.

Let me say this clearly: God doesn't fill you just for you. He doesn't pour out His Spirit just to make church services more exciting. The end goal of a Spirit-activated life is that the reign of Jesus would be seen and felt everywhere your life touches. Our Savior didn't tell us to pray, "Get me out of here and into heaven as fast as possible." Instead, He taught us these words: "Your kingdom come, your will be done, on earth as it is in heaven" (Matthew 6:10). The vision of the kingdom is more than a better you or a better church. It's bringing heaven into your workplace, your family, your community, your calling, your industry, and anywhere else you have influence.

Church vs. Kingdom

Much has been written about the difference between the local church, the global Church, and the kingdom of God. Here's a simple way I frame it:

- The **local church** is the spiritual family where you're known, cared for, corrected, discipled, and activated. It's the actual people you lock arms with, serve beside, and grow with (*not* your favorite podcast or the preacher you follow online).

- The **global Church** is the collective body of Christ across every tribe, nation, and tongue. It reminds us that we're part of something bigger than our zip code.

- The **kingdom of God** is wherever the rule and reign of Jesus breaks through with justice, mercy, mission, generosity, and love. It's the influence of Spirit-filled believers bringing heaven's values into earthly spaces.

Yes, the kingdom is bigger than the Church, but it's not separate from it. Kingdom impact begins in you, gets formed in community, and then flows into the world. You can't bypass the middle step.

When Kingdom Comes Through One Life

Ryan and Jessica are friends of mine who run a design firm in Dallas, Texas. As a dynamic duo, these two are truly a creative force, and as brilliant strategists, they are deeply respected in their industry.

For years, Ryan and Jessica kept their faith separate from their professional life. They'd say things like, "We do church on Sunday, but we don't bring it into the workplace." But that changed when God started stirring something deeper in them. The couple went through a difficult season of church burnout, and they disappeared for several months, almost quitting altogether.

But instead of walking away, Ryan and Jessica spoke to a veteran kingdom business builder who was fully devoted to leading their twenty-million-dollar company for the glory of God in every way possible. The couple submitted their vision to God in prayer, stayed rooted in faith, found a new church, and began asking, *What if we brought our whole selves into every space, with creativity, faith, AND Spirit? What if God's vision for our business is bigger than our vision? What if what we do in our work is actually worship?*

Today, their business is what I call a "kingdom business." It's committed to God, for His glory. Superbloom has an even greater meaning now. Meetings begin with prayer, whether the room is full of believers or not. Employees know the owners genuinely love them. Ryan and Jessica even started mentoring young creatives, not just in career goals but in kingdom vision too. They fund church multiplication and global missions.

The couple works harder than ever so they can invest even more in the kingdom. And recently, one of their longtime coworkers gave their life to Jesus and said, "You guys live like God is real, not just on Sunday but everywhere." That, my friends, is a kingdom superbloom.

How to Live in a Kingdom Superbloom

Here are three practical ways to take what God is doing in you and bring it into the spaces where you live, work, and lead.

1. BRING THE SAME SURRENDER INTO EVERY ROOM

Stop compartmentalizing your faith. The same Spirit who speaks to you in worship wants to speak through you in meetings, in parenting, in classroom conversations, and in unexpected interruptions. Don't shrink God down to church language. Invite Him into your ordinary life and let your obedience echo in public spaces.

2. LET YOUR LOCAL CHURCH REFINE AND SEND YOU

Stay planted and accountable. Don't disconnect from the body God uses to shape you. Your local church isn't perfect, but neither are you. Let it be the training ground, the family table, and the launchpad for your most healthy kingdom impact. Isolation leads to distortion, but community leads to clarity.

3. ASK, "WHERE CAN THE KINGDOM BREAK IN THROUGH ME TODAY?"

This mindset shift will change your life. Don't wait for a pulpit to preach or a mission trip to live on mission. The Spirit of God in you is ready to heal, encourage, create, speak, and love through you today. Ask, *Lord, who do You want to bless through my obedience today? How do You want to show up through me in this room?*

The superbloom God wants to release through you was never meant to stay inside a sanctuary. It was meant to spill into boardrooms, schools, neighborhoods, phone calls, dinner tables, and broken places. You are a carrier of the kingdom, and the bloom He planted in you is meant to be seen.

If this feels a bit too much right now, I encourage you to stick with me. In the next chapter, I will go deeper into the sincere roots of faith and explore what's actually in the soil of your heart. I hope to see you there!

The superbloom God wants to release through you was never meant to stay inside a sanctuary.

CHAPTER 1 STUDY GUIDE

If the Spirit of him who raised Jesus from the dead is living in you, he who raised Christ from the dead will also give life to your mortal bodies because of his Spirit who lives in you.

—**Romans 8:11**

REVIEW

A superbloom is a spiritual awakening that happens when God's Word meets the Holy Spirit's power in a believer's life. This isn't about access (getting more of God) but about activation, as God gets more of us through surrendered minds, wills, and emotions.

Spiritual growth requires both God's Word (the seed) and the Holy Spirit (the rain) working together. Without God's Word, believers can be emotionally driven but unstable (soaked but seedless). Without the Holy Spirit, they can be theologically informed but spiritually dry (Word-rich but rain-starved). The Spirit empowers what the Word reveals, and the Word forms what the Spirit fills. Neither is effective alone, but when combined, spiritual growth becomes inevitable.

Ministry strategies must never replace authentic encounters with God's presence and power. When growth techniques become the focus, they lure leaders away from pure devotion to Jesus, causing distraction and compromise. But when we return to the pure seed of God's Word, we witness the natural results of abiding in His love and partnering with Him to change His world. A personal superbloom reflects what God awakens in you, a corporate superbloom manifests when believers gather in surrender, and a kingdom superbloom overflows through us into the world.

KEY SCRIPTURES

The Spirit gives life; the flesh counts for nothing. The words I have spoken to you—they are full of the Spirit and life. (John 6:63)

Now to him who is able to do immeasurably more than all we ask or imagine, according to his power that is at work within us. (Ephesians 3:20)

Faith *comes* from hearing, and hearing by the word of Christ. (Romans 10:17 NASB)

This is to my Father's glory, that you bear much fruit, showing yourselves to be my disciples. (John 15:8)

PERSONAL REFLECTION

1. What dreams, callings, or giftings have you written off as "dead"? What would it look like for God to awaken those dormant seeds?

2. What would it look like to create intentional rhythms of stillness in your daily schedule, and what might be the biggest obstacle?

3. Before attending your next church service or gathering, how will you prepare to be a contributor and "wake up the room"?

4. What areas of your life (work, relationships, hobbies, etc.) remain separate from your faith, and how will you invite God's presence there this week?

PRAYER

Father God, thank You that Your Spirit lives within us with the same mighty power that raised Jesus from the dead. Today, we surrender all anxieties, ambitions, and agendas that keep us from experiencing the fullness of Your presence. Awaken what is dormant within us, Lord. Let real rain fall on the real seed of Your Word in our hearts. Where we are full of knowledge but spiritually dry, breathe fresh life. Where we are emotional but rootless, plant Your truth deep within our spirit. May what You're doing in us overflow into our communities and workplaces, and may the watching world see Your presence everywhere we go. In Jesus' name, Amen.

2

SINCERE FAITH

The Holy Spirit is not an add-on to the Christian life.
He is the Christian life.

—Author Unknown

I planted the seed, Apollos watered it, but God has been making it grow.
—1 Corinthians 3:6

A Superbloom needs three things to appear: seed, soil and water. Worship and prayer are the H20 that activates the seed planted in the soil of the believer.

—Paul Wilbur

THERE'S NO GREATER gift you can experience from God than a sincere and pure conscience. This is not attained by effort or will power nor is it attained without them. It's a gift of grace from God granting you sincere faith and a tender heart as a home for Him. Love and obedience are formed in this sincere and pure place of faith.

I was twelve years old when I first understood what sincere faith looked like in real life. I was sitting in my dad's worn leather chair, and his Bible lay open beside me. It was heavily marked with notes, highlighted verses, and the kind of wear that comes from decades of daily use. Behind his chair stood two bookshelves packed with Christian books, Bible commentaries, and notebooks from seminars he'd attended, sacrificing time and money to grow deeper in his understanding of God's Word.

Ronald Jenkins has never been a pastor. He is a jack of all trades and a master of sincere faith. He was saved and baptized after a heavy run of rebellion, a Vietnam tour with two purple hearts and a bronze star, and deep soul searching in his early twenties. When Dad surrendered to Christ, it meant stepping up in the heavyweight division of faith, trust, and responsibility. It would be impossible to list all the ways he sacrificed for my mom and his three sons. His faithfulness was (and is) truly remarkable.

Dad worked sixty-plus hours a week to provide for our family as a superintendent for a natural gas company. "Working overtime" was a phrase said in our home almost every week. Yet Dad was also the most consistent student of Scripture I knew. He drove home every single day with a coworker named Vernon Clay, who did not know the Lord, and we heard him talk to Vernon about Jesus almost every day. They ate sandwiches or leftovers from the night before and drank sweet tea at our kitchen table every day with us.

Our family had breakfast together before work and school every day. We ate dinner together every day too. Dad always led us in prayer and conversation. With grit and loyalty, he kept us going through Mom's chronic health challenges and more than fifty surgeries that disrupted our lives repeatedly.

Dad persevered, doing whatever needed to be done. He kept serving, cooking, working, building, training, teaching, leading, loving, and nurturing us. Every single night, he was the one who came to our beds, prayed with us, and blessed us. He was and still is a man of sincere faith.

Note that phrase: sincere faith. Dad was never too tired to father us. He never led us to skip church. He was never too busy to attend Bible classes, Bible study, or worship services. He found a way to put his three sons through private Christian school and laid his life down to pass on the sincere faith that burned in his heart.

Dad gave me hunger for the Word, hospitality, love for people, and faithful service. He's the reason I pastor the way I do today. That's what happens when sincere faith lives not just in your mind but in the depths of your being. Yes, it changes you, but it also creates a generational superbloom that impacts people you'll never meet.

Many believers today are trying to build what my dad gave me from scratch. They're attempting to create in one generation what's designed to be cultivated through time and legacy. They wonder why their spiritual life feels so effortful, why they struggle with consistency, and why they can't seem to grasp the kind of faith they see in others.

The answer might not be trying harder. It might be understanding what sincere faith actually is and how it gets passed down.

WHAT IS SINCERE FAITH?

I am still learning this and I've learned most of it the hard way. I never cognitively doubted God one single time until I was twenty-three years old and in my second year of graduate school studying theology. I quickly went from having a childlike faith to deeply troubled doubts. I wasn't a hypocrite, but the level of uncertainty I experienced was surfacing from a faith soil layered with strongholds of fear, insecurity, broken thinking, sin, and shame.

Doubting God emotionally is usually in your soil long before you experience doubts cognitively.

I don't know if Timothy experienced the same kind of fear or insecurity I did, but he apparently had enough trouble inside him that the apostle Paul thought it necessary to remind him of the sincere faith in him, his grandmother, and his mother. This led me to consider that faith is not the absence of doubt but the certainty of what you hope for in the absence of sight. The opposite of faith is not doubt. The opposite of faith is sight.

That's huge.

Many leaders and influencers push a faith without doubt, but I don't think that's a realistic way to grow. Sincere faith, according to my experience, is a cultivated certainty rooted in simplicity, pure trust, obedience, and repentance. We keep moving toward our great hope despite doubts and even onslaughts of unbelief.

In Matthew 21:22, Jesus tells us what's possible if we believe and do not doubt: "If you believe, you will receive whatever you ask for in prayer."

When Paul wrote his final letter to Timothy from a Roman prison cell, he didn't waste words on ministry strategies or theological abstractions. He went straight to the foundation that would influence how Timothy would survive the crushing pressures ahead:

> I am reminded of your sincere faith, which first lived in your grandmother Lois and in your mother Eunice and, I am persuaded, now lives in you also. For this reason I remind you to fan into flame the gift of God, which is in you. (2 Timothy 1:5–6)

Sitting in my dad's chair as a twelve-year-old, looking at his marked-up Bible and those shelves of Christian books behind me, I witnessed what Paul called *anupokritos pistis* (sincere faith).

The Greek word *anupokritos* literally means 'without hypocrisy' or 'unfeigned.' It's the same root from which we get *hypocrite*, but with a negating prefix that completely reverses the meaning. A hypocrite was originally a stage actor who wore masks to play different characters, speaking lines written by others. Sincere faith is the exact opposite. Instead of a semi-compliant performance borrowed from someone else's script, sincere faith is authentic devotion that emerges from your genuine relationship with God through understanding, obedience, and repentance.

My dad's faith wasn't inherited religiosity or cultural Christianity. It was a living, breathing relationship with God that survived sixty-hour work weeks, my mom's chronic health challenges, and the mundane pressures of raising three boys. He didn't just believe in Jesus intellectually. He surrendered his life completely to Christ, and that surrender shaped every decision, sacrifice, and quiet moment in his chair with that worn Bible. This is where a spiritual superbloom begins: not with perfect or impressive faith but with sincere faith.

Paul presents sincere faith as both a divine gift and human responsibility. Notice the flow in his letter: The sincere faith that "lives in you" (God's gift) leads directly to "fan into flame" (your responsibility). This reveals the beautiful tension of authentic spirituality. God plants genuine faith as His unmerited favor, *and* we're called to cultivate what He's given. Sincere faith is a living seed that requires intentional tending.

This is where a spiritual superbloom begins: not with perfect or impressive faith but with sincere faith.

Sincere Faith	vs.	Performative Faith
Source: The Spirit and the Word of God		Source: Borrowed from family/culture
Motivation: Love for God		Motivation: Approval from people
Consistency: Same in private and public		Consistency: Changes with audience
Foundation: Word of God in heart		Foundation: Cultural expectations
Under Pressure: Deepens and strengthens		Under Pressure: Compromises
Evidence: Character transformation		Evidence: External charisma
Result: Reproduces in others		Result: Creates dependency
Sustainability: Outlives circumstances		Sustainability: Needs validation

When Scripture talks about saving faith, it describes this kind of authentic, life-surrendering trust. In Ephesians 2:8, Paul writes, "For by grace you have been saved through faith" (ESV). In Romans 10:9–10, he shows that genuine faith both speaks ("confess with your mouth") and believes ("in your heart") (ESV). But Paul goes further in 2 Corinthians 13:5 when he challenges believers to "examine yourselves, to see whether you are in the faith" (ESV).

Why would he say that?

Because there's a kind of hollow faith that has no saving power and certainly no supernatural manifestation. Instead, it's a cultural Christianity with inherited religiosity and spiritual image management. You cannot bypass authentic devotion, genuine worship, surrender, and repentance, and still expect spiritual results.

Paul puts it perfectly in Galatians 5:6: "The only thing that counts is faith expressing itself through love." That's not a mushy t-shirt slogan. That's the Spirit of truth. When sincere faith takes root, it produces spiritual fruit that synthetic faith never can. Sincere faith survives intense fire (see 1 Peter 1:7), stands through trials, and produces righteousness that transforms not just you but others around you too.

MEET LOIS, EUNICE, AND TIMOTHY

Lois and Eunice didn't just teach Timothy about faith; they also modeled what faith looks like when it breathes. They lived with such authentic devotion that it became part of Timothy's spiritual DNA. When Paul met this young man, the apostle recognized the same genuine spiritual substance that characterized the women who raised him.

Here's the key connection: The Holy Spirit doesn't work around sincere faith or despite its absence. He works through it. Consider this the crucial question: "Does God give you his Spirit and work miracles among you by the works of the law, or by your believing what you heard?" (Galatians 3:5). The Spirit of God responds to simple faith, authentic surrender, and genuine devotion that lives in you, whether anyone else is watching or not.

If you're wondering why you haven't experienced a personal superbloom, set aside your resume and check your roots. Please pay careful attention to this: You can copy what others do and get results that look successful. Even Paul says some preach Christ out of selfish ambition, and I'm sure there was real impact that resulted in others finding salvation. However, if you do this, your work will be shown for what it is. Paul says fire will test it and prove that it's empty.

If you want lasting impact, you need sincere faith as your foundation.

- You cannot fake your way into true spiritual authority.

- You cannot manufacture anointing through techniques and programs.

- You cannot skip over the foundation and expect supernatural results.

The Spirit is looking for genuine soil to work in, real faith to activate, and authentic devotion to empower with gifts and manifestations.

At the heart of every personal superbloom is the truth that the Spirit activates what's already planted inside you. The supernatural manifestation, the spiritual gifts, the power, the love, and the self-discipline all flow from the foundation of authentic, unfeigned, sincere faith.

The Holy Spirit never skips over sincere faith.

He activates it.

The Tree That Takes Eighty Years

During one of my trips to Israel, my favorite guide, Arie Bar David, taught biblical botany like I had never heard. He's who introduced me to something that forever changed how I understand spiritual legacy. We were studying olive trees and their three pressings when he mentioned another tree that caught my attention: the tamarisk tree.

"You don't just stumble upon a tamarisk tree," Arie explained. "Each one was intentionally planted and carefully cultivated. It's what we call the legacy tree."

The tamarisk tree is remarkable for several reasons:

- It was deliberately planted as a sign of covenant or faithfulness.

- It thrives in harsh, salty, desert conditions where few trees survive.

- It grows slowly, sometimes taking decades to reach full maturity.

- Once mature, it provides cool, dense shade, offering rare relief in the desert heat.

What captured my heart most is that tamarisk trees were planted not for yourself but for generations to come, even those you may never meet.

Abraham planted the first recorded tamarisk tree in Genesis 21:33, calling on "the name of the Lord, the Everlasting God" (ESV) beneath its branches. This father of the faith understood something we've forgotten in our instant-gratification culture: The most valuable things in life require generational thinking.

This is exactly what Paul was describing when he wrote to Timothy about Lois and Eunice. The apostle wasn't making pleasant, idle conversation about family heritage. Paul was on his deathbed, writing one last letter to his spiritual son who needed to hear that what was in him was sincere and well-rooted generationally.

You cannot fake your way into true spiritual authority.

THREE LEVELS OF SINCERE FAITH

Paul reveals something profound in 2 Timothy 1:5 about how sincere faith develops across generations. He shows us three distinct levels of legacy faith, each essential for spiritual superbloom.

Level 1: The Lois Level (OG Faith)

You probably know that in the hip-hop world, "OG" stands for "Original Gangster." Well, the first level of legacy faith is what I call "OG Faith": the original, authentic, personal devotion that establishes you as a pioneer rather than a copy. Everyone needs this and to know their own faith. Lois was an original, not a fake. She represents the believers who refuse to live on borrowed faith or manufactured spirituality.

Picture this: Paul has just finished preaching in the marketplace of Lystra when the crowd turns violent. Within minutes, they're dragging him outside the city gates, throwing stones until they think he's dead. Then something amazing happens: "After the disciples had gathered around him, he got up" (Acts 14:20).

There was no established church in Lystra yet. These disciples were brand new converts who had just heard the gospel for the first time and surrendered their lives to Jesus. I'm convinced Lois was right there in that circle, one of the believers kneeling around Paul's bloodied body.

Imagine what that took. As a Jewish woman living in a hostile Roman colony, Lois's conversion to Christianity wasn't just spiritually significant; it was also physically dangerous and socially costly. She had just seen what happened to the man who preached this gospel. Yet something about what she'd heard was so authentic, so life-changing, that she was willing to risk everything for it.

This is what real OG faith looks like: You encounter truth so genuine that you'll bet your life on it, even when everyone around you thinks you're crazy. Lois became a founding member of the church in Lystra, establishing spiritual territory that would impact the world through her grandson Timothy.

The first century church was loaded with OGs. In every city the apostles entered, genuine conversions took place as men and women sincerely surrendered their whole lives to the gospel of Jesus Christ.

Meet Lydia

My favorite example of OG faith in Scripture is Lydia from Acts 16. When Paul arrived in Philippi, he expected to find a synagogue with men leading prayer and devotion. Instead, he encountered some women gathered by a river for prayer. This is significant. It took only ten to twelve men to form a synagogue, so there were no (or very few) Jewish men in this major city.

But there was Lydia. The Bible describes her as "a dealer in purple cloth" (successful marketplace leader) and "a worshipper of God" (authentic devotional life) (v. 14). Lydia didn't need a building, a pastor, or a crowd to maintain her devotion. Her professional success flowed from something deeper.

As Lydia listened to Paul preach, "the Lord opened her heart to respond" (Acts 16:14). Here's the progression that reveals how OG faith works:

- God opened Lydia's heart (divine initiative).

- She responded (human responsibility).

- She was baptized (public declaration).

- She opened her home (immediate kingdom impact).

When the Lord opens your heart, it's OG time. You can't decide to have sincere faith, but when God offers it, you can receive it fully rather than settling for surface-level religion. When you do, it changes you *and* transforms everything around you.

What was inside Lydia was also manifesting around her. Yes, her faith was personal, but it also created a spiritual atmosphere that impacted her entire household and ultimately established the church in Philippi. Two thousand years later, you can visit that spot in Philippi and find a church and amphitheater built to commemorate where an OG once lived.

Key OG Faith Scriptures

Faith comes from hearing the message, and the message is heard through the word about Christ. (Romans 10:17)

I have been crucified with Christ and I no longer live, but Christ lives in me. (Galatians 2:20)

If anyone is in Christ, the new creation has come. (2 Corinthians 5:17)

Three Barriers to OG Faith (and How to Break Through)

Developing OG faith isn't automatic. After years of ministry, I've identified three barriers that keep people stuck in surface-level Christianity instead of authentic devotion.

BARRIER #1: APPROVAL ADDICTION

The need for validation from others to feel spiritually secure is common. The problem comes when your faith rises and falls based on other's approval, your family's expectations, or your church community's recognition.

Breakthrough: Submit to pure daily devotion. Spend time with God every day that no one knows about. Don't post about it on social media and don't share about it in small group. When your private relationship with Jesus matters more than your public spiritual reputation, you're developing OG faith. It is truly aimed at Him as the highest pleasure and goal.

BARRIER #2: COMFORT ZONE CHRISTIANITY

You want Jesus as Savior but resist Him as Lord. There are likely many strongholds in your life that fuel unhealthy comfort routines. You avoid repentance and lean heavily into security, but you won't surrender areas of control, comfort, or personal ambition. This leads to powerless religion.

Breakthrough: Practice radical obedience and repentance in one specific area this week. Surrender your finances, relationships, entertainment choices, or career decisions. OG faith grows through progressive surrender and repentance, not massive spiritual overhauls.

BARRIER #3: INSTANT RESULTS EXPECTATIONS

You want spiritual breakthrough without patient cultivation. You expect supernatural gifts without character development and spiritual authority without faithful service in hidden places. You have a form of godliness, but you are void when it comes to discipline, self-control, and patience.

Breakthrough: Commit to one spiritual discipline for six months without measuring visible results. Read Scripture daily, pray consistently, or serve faithfully in an unglamorous role. OG faith develops through patient investment and a thousand small surrenders that no one else will ever see. There are no spiritual shortcuts.

The beautiful truth is God doesn't require perfect or impressive faith to begin working in your life. He just needs sincere faith. Do you have authentic, honest devotion that's willing to grow? Your OG faith journey starts with one honest prayer: "God, I want the real thing. Whatever it costs, whatever it requires, I want authentic faith that lives in me." Get this on repeat in your heart.

Level 2: The Eunice Level (The Steward)

The second level of legacy faith moves from establishing authentic faith to protecting and cultivating it through seasons of opposition, boredom, and spiritual attack. This is where many believers struggle. They experience genuine conversion but fail to develop the disciplines necessary to steward what God has planted.

Stewarding faith protects and cultivates the seed through seasons of testing and opposition. To understand what this requires, you need to grasp the courage Eunice demonstrated daily. Everyone in Lystra knew what happened to Paul, the man who preached about Jesus and was stoned and left for dead (Acts 14:19–20). Eunice wasn't just raising Timothy in a spiritually hostile environment; she was also discipling him in the very place where following Jesus had nearly cost a man his life. Every day, she had to choose between her safety and her son's spiritual development.

The challenges Eunice navigated would defeat most modern Christians:

- **Cultural Opposition**—She lived in a Roman culture that demanded the worship of Caesar while maintaining Jewish practices and an authentic OG Christian conversion.

- **Marriage Isolation**—Acts 16:3 reveals, "They all knew that his father was a Greek," meaning this was a prominent family under public scrutiny. Eunice had to maintain her faith while married to someone who likely viewed her Christian conversion as a dangerous rebellion against both Roman culture and family stability.

- **Public Pressure**—As part of a well-known mixed-heritage family, Eunice knew everyone in Lystra and surrounding cities watched how she raised Timothy, creating constant social pressure to conform rather than convert.

- **Spiritual Isolation**—Essentially a single mother in spiritual terms, she carried the entire burden of Timothy's spiritual development without institutional support, pastoral guidance, or community reinforcement.

- **Long-term Vision**—Eunice planted spiritual seeds in her son that she might not live to see flourish, while navigating a cultural identity crisis between Jewish heritage, Greek marriage, and Christian faith.

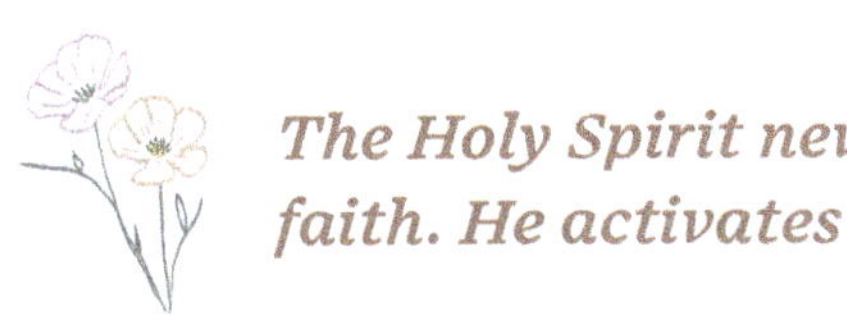

The Holy Spirit never skips over sincere faith. He activates it.

In 2 Timothy 3:15, Paul reveals that "from infancy" Timothy has "known the Holy Scriptures." Eunice was intentional about getting God's Word into her son's heart from birth. She understood that stewardship means fighting to protect the seed, the soil, and the atmosphere of faith regardless of external circumstances.

This is exactly what every parent trying to raise godly children in an ungodly culture understands. Every wife whose husband doesn't share her spiritual passion knows Eunice's isolation. Every believer who's the only Christian in their workplace feels her courage. Eunice-level faith is more than ancient history. It's the daily reality of anyone choosing to steward authentic faith in a hostile environment.

The Salt Crystal Protection

The tamarisk tree offers a powerfully theological metaphor. Mature tamarisk trees excrete salt crystals on their branches that serve dual purposes: preservation and protection. When wind or rain carry these crystals to the ground, the soil beneath the tree changes. The increased salinity discourages weeds and competing plants, creating a protected zone around the tree's roots that shields what's life-giving and prevents what could choke it out.

This botanical process represents how mature faith develops supernatural protection. Your devotion to God's Word creates an environment where spiritual life is maintained. The "salt" of your character preserves the spiritual atmosphere around you, and your commitment to holiness repels influences that would corrupt your heart.

Jesus told His followers, "You are the salt of the earth" (Matthew 5:13). When you develop Eunice-level faith, you become salt in your environment, preserving the good, purifying the contaminated, and making following Jesus attractive to others.

Salt	Spiritual Application
Preservation	Keeps what is pure from corruption
Flavor	Makes life more appealing and satisfying
Covenant	Lasts forever and doesn't decay
Purification	Cleanses what's been contaminated

The steward level requires developing salt crystal character through consistent spiritual disciplines, even (and especially) when no one else supports your choices. Paul's letters to Timothy reveal what this looks like:

Watch your life and doctrine closely. Persevere in them.
(1 Timothy 4:16)

Guard the good deposit that was entrusted to you.
(2 Timothy 1:14)

Present yourself to God as one approved, a worker who does not need to be ashamed. (2 Timothy 2:15)

I have fought the good fight, I have finished the race, I have kept the faith. (2 Timothy 4:7)

The question isn't whether you'll face opposition to your faith. You certainly will. The question is whether you'll develop the salt crystal character that not only survives pressure but actually uses it to protect and preserve what God is growing in and around you. This is how sincere faith moves from personal authenticity to generational impact.

Level 3: The Timothy Level (The Multiplier)

Picture a nervous young man getting a message that would change his life forever. Paul, the most famous missionary in the world, has written: *Timothy, I need you. There's a crisis in Thessalonica, and you're the only one I trust to handle it.*

This wasn't a one-time thing. Every time Paul faced his toughest assignments, whether churches in chaos, false teachers spreading lies, or communities on the verge of collapse, he sent Timothy. Not Peter, not Barnabas, not any of the other apostles. Timothy. The young man who started in his grandmother's living room became Paul's secret weapon.

What I love about Timothy's story is that he didn't start with a lot of confidence, and God knows I didn't either. Paul had to keep encouraging Timothy to "fan into flame the gift of God" (2 Timothy 1:6), to stop letting people intimidate him because he was young, and to embrace the power that was already inside him.

- Even Timothy needed pep talks.

- Even Timothy battled insecurity.

- Even Timothy needed to be reminded of what was already planted within him.

The sincere faith that began in Lois and Eunice didn't just survive in Timothy. It exploded through him. He became the catalyst for church multiplication throughout the entire province of Asia. He trained leaders who trained other leaders. He planted churches that planted churches. If Lois and Eunice were the roots, Timothy was the harvest that kept producing more harvests.

This is the Timothy Level: moving from protecting what you've received to intentionally reproducing it in others.

- You stop measuring spiritual success by what you're getting and start measuring it by who you're raising up.

- You become someone who doesn't just attend church but helps create churches.

- You don't just consume ministry. You multiply ministers.

The goal of every spiritual superbloom is simple: take what you've been given and cause it to multiply in others. That's how one grandmother's prayers in Lystra eventually influenced the entire Roman Empire. That's how your sincere faith today can impact people you'll never meet.

When Paul wrote his final letter to Timothy, the apostle was on his deathbed, about to be martyred. In that context, he gave instructions that would determine whether the gospel would survive or die with his generation: "And the things you have heard me say in the presence of many witnesses entrust to reliable people who will also be qualified to teach others" (2 Timothy 2:2).

Notice the four generations of multiplication:

- Christ → Paul (divine revelation to apostle)

- Paul → Timothy (apostle to spiritual son)

- Timothy → Reliable people (spiritual son to faithful leaders)

- Reliable people → Others (faithful leaders to new disciples)

This is more than church growth strategy. It's the divine design for how authentic faith spreads throughout the earth.

Timothy was pastoring the church in Ephesus, the most influential congregation in Asia. Biblical evidence suggests that he became the greatest church multiplier in the New Testament, establishing and overseeing churches throughout the entire province. More than just a popular figurehead, Timothy multiplied his ministry by reproducing himself in others.

The Power of Exponential Multiplication

Addition builds programs; multiplication builds movements. With addition, you could witness to ten people, and the result is ten new followers of Jesus. But with multiplication, you could disciple two people who each disciple many others and so on. That result is exponential growth over time.

Key Multiplication Scriptures

> Go and make disciples of all nations ... teaching them to obey everything I have commanded you. (Matthew 28:19–20)

> To equip his people for works of service, so that the body of Christ may be built up. (Ephesians 4:11–12)

> I have sent you Timothy, my son whom I love, who is faithful in the Lord. (1 Corinthians 4:17)

When you move beyond consumer Christianity to become a multiplier, you invest in reliable people who will invest in others, creating exponential rather than addition-based growth. You stop being a spiritual consumer and become a spiritual reproducer.

Our goal cannot be limited to adding disciples.

We must multiply disciple-makers.

Legacy Is Not What You Leave Behind

Mike Nevil is a hero in the faith to me. His daughter, Celeste, and her husband, Andrew, have been a part of our foundation team from the beginning. Andrew is the Director/President of Mission Maasai, and I serve on the board with him. We're serving the vision that God gave Pastor Timothy Moilo in Kenya.

How?

The way Mike Nevil has done it from the beginning.

Mike visited the bush village of Empukani, Kenya, several decades ago. He helped a young pastor named Timothy establish his new church and built the first building. For decades, Mike labored in removing barriers that hinder kingdom growth. While he was alive, we helped thirty-one churches start. Every church began under an Acacia tree. (We'll discuss that tree in the next chapter.) We built a large base church building, a seminary, and a lodge. We have trained more than fifty more pastors and helped many of them start new churches.

Mike passed away in 2024, but his legacy is just getting started. We now have dozens more churches ready to plant and more pastors needing training in our seminary than we're able to facilitate. Mike lived with a tamarisk mentality, as he planted trees he'd never enjoy the shade of.

I can't think of a better superbloom.

So how do you develop such a legacy mindset?

- Your daily time in Scripture becomes more than personal development. It becomes the preservative that protects your family's spiritual atmosphere.

- Your prayer life becomes more than personal comfort. It becomes purification that cleanses the environment around you.

- Your character becomes more than personal integrity. It becomes salt that makes following Jesus attractive to others.

- Your intentional investment is relational, deep, pastoral, and loaded with a shepherding heart for generational impact.

For those on the outside looking in, those points might sound like legalistic rule-keeping. But in reality, they are the natural results of authentic faith cultivated over time. When wind blows those salt crystals to the ground, they kill everything that would harm the tree while preserving everything that contributes to its health.

When the pressures of life blow against your mature faith, what comes out protects rather than destroys, preserves rather than corrupts, and multiplies rather than diminishes. This is how one person's sincere faith can impact generations they'll never meet.

The Spirit of God is waiting to activate what you're willing to cultivate with generational vision.

YOUR LEGACY TREE STARTS TODAY

As I write this chapter, I'm acutely aware that I'm planting seeds for descendants I may never meet. The faith I'm cultivating today, the disciplines I'm establishing now, and the people I'm investing in currently are all part of a legacy tree that will either provide shade or cast shadows for generations to come.

The same is true for you. Whether you're twenty or seventy, single or married, a parent or childless, you're creating spiritual inheritance for people whose names you don't yet know. The sincere faith you develop today will help determine the spiritual resources available to those who come after you.

You don't need perfect circumstances to start planting your legacy tree.

- Abraham planted his tamarisk in the desert.

- Lois established faith in a hostile culture.

- Eunice protected spiritual development despite family opposition.

- Timothy multiplied disciples during persecution.

What they all had in common wasn't ideal conditions but sincere faith that lived within them and flowed out to others.

Revival always starts with individuals

- who refuse to settle for anything less than the real thing;

- who commit to the patient work of cultivating authentic faith; and

- who understand that what they plant today determines what future generations harvest tomorrow.

Your legacy tree is ready to be planted. The soil of your heart is prepared. The seed of God's Word is available. The Spirit of God is waiting to activate what you're willing to cultivate with generational vision.

DAD

A few weeks ago, I got a call from Dad. He was in an ambulance headed to the hospital. He's seventy-six years old and had a quadruple bypass back in 2012. Since that surgery, he's had numerous episodes that required a pacemaker, a new medication, or some form of upgrade on his "ticker."

This time, his blood counts were very low, and he needed a transfusion. I immediately left McKinney to be with him. He's fine now. I'm grateful.

Every time we talk, we talk about the Lord and the ministry Dad is doing. Mom passed at the age of sixty-five, and eventually, Dad remarried. He and his wife, Sherry, now live on a thirty-acre crawfish farm surrounded by huge Spanish-moss-covered oak trees in southern Louisiana. It's beautiful.

Dad and Sherry really have such a great time together. They've built multiple farm-related buildings, multiple tables, an outdoor kitchen, and an outdoor extended patio. They sit on their front porch facing a massive front yard and harvest the squirrels that mess with their pecan trees. (Yes, they eat the squirrels in sauce piquant or gumbo.) They raise chickens and keep a basket on the counter full of eggs. They garden together, fish together, and worship together.

Dad and Sherry are involved in a church near their house. One day the pastor said, "Ron, I need you to help me disciple some of these younger men. Will you pray about taking over that ministry?"

At seventy-five years old, Dad said *yes*.

Why? He has sincere faith.

He's still cultivating his legacy tree. He loves the Lord. He loves his wife. He loves his family. He's such a good and faithful man.

It's not about show or goals or success. It's just pure, sincere faith. I want more of that. I'm still taking notes on how my dad cultivates it, but this is what I know: The superbloom starts with sincere faith, and sincere faith starts with simplicity.

CHAPTER 2 STUDY GUIDE

The goal of this command is love, which comes from a pure heart and a good conscience and a sincere faith.

—1 Timothy 1:5

REVIEW

Sincere faith (*anupokritos pistis*) is the essential foundation for spiritual superbloom. It reveals authentic devotion born from a genuine relationship with God through understanding, obedience, and repentance. Rather than the absence of doubt, sincere faith is the certainty of what we hope for even when we cannot see.

In 2 Timothy 1:5–6, Paul reveals three levels of legacy faith to show how sincere faith develops across generations. Level 1: The Lois Level (OG Faith) represents the original devotion that makes you a pioneer, not a copy. God opens your heart, and you respond with surrender, creating spiritual territory that impacts the world. Level 2: The Eunice Level (The Steward) preserves spiritual life and resists corruption. You protect and cultivate faith even through opposition, boredom, and spiritual attack. Level 3: The Timothy Level (The Multiplier) moves from preservation to reproduction. You measure success by those you're raising up, pursuing exponential multiplication over addition.

Like Abraham's tamarisk, your legacy tree is ready to be planted. The soil of your heart is prepared. The seed of God's Word is available. The sincere faith you nurture today will determine the spiritual inheritance of generations to come.

KEY SCRIPTURES

I am reminded of your sincere faith, which first lived in your grandmother Lois and in your mother Eunice and now lives in you also. For this reason I remind you to fan into flame the gift of God, which is in you. (2 Timothy 1:5–6)

Faith comes from hearing the message, and the message is heard through the word about Christ. (Romans 10:17)

For by grace you have been saved through faith. (Ephesians 2:8 ESV)

The only thing that counts is faith expressing itself through love. (Galatians 5:6)

GROUP DISCUSSION

1. What are the visible differences between someone living with authentic devotion versus someone performing borrowed scripts? How can we recognize these patterns in our own lives?

2. Paul presents sincere faith as both divine gift and human responsibility ("lives in you" and "fan into flame"). How do we balance the tension between what God plants and what we must cultivate?

3. What are the unique challenges and temptations at each level of legacy faith: OG, Steward, Multiplier?

4. What is the difference between faith that deepens under pressure and faith that crumbles or compromises? What can we learn from Eunice's stewardship in hostile environments?

5. Why do many churches struggle to develop multipliers rather than just accumulate consumers? How can we encourage believers to cultivate spiritual disciplines that may not show visible results for years?

PERSONAL REFLECTION

1. What evidence would someone find of your authentic devotion to God if they examined your private spiritual life?

2. The three barriers to OG faith are Approval Addiction, Comfort Zone Christianity, and Instant Results Expectations. Which barrier most accurately describes your current spiritual struggle, and what specific breakthrough step will you implement this week to address it?

3. How does your current approach to spiritual disciplines demonstrate legacy thinking? What choices are you making today that will create spiritual inheritance for future generations?

4. What would shift in your spiritual life if you measured success by whom you're raising up rather than what you're consuming or achieving?

PRAYER

Father God, thank You for the gift of sincere faith. Plant in us the kind of OG faith that encounters truth so genuine we'll bet our lives on it. Give us Eunice-level courage to steward and protect what You've planted, even in hostile environments. Raise us to be like Timothy, so that we multiply disciple-makers rather than just consume ministry. We want to have salt crystal character that preserves the spiritual atmosphere and makes following Jesus attractive to others. Give us generational vision to invest in people whose names we don't yet know. May our sincere faith live, breathe, survive, and produce fruit for Your glory. In Jesus' name, Amen.

3

TOTAL GIFT PACKAGE

The Spirit without the Word is blind enthusiasm; the Word without the Spirit is dead orthodoxy.

—Dr. Martyn Lloyd-Jones

Faith does not operate in the realm of the possible. There is no glory for God in that which is humanly possible. Faith begins where man's power ends.

—George Muller

I STOOD IN the middle of Glacier National Park. I was on a hike, and a powerful waterfall overwhelmed the atmosphere at one point on the trail. It was just after sunrise, and the sun lit up the rocks around it like it had something to prove. Purple shadows, gold streaks, pink mist curling along jagged cliffs that stretched farther than my eyes could track. The roar was its own kind of music. My whole body lit up.

I took one picture and texted it to my family with the caption, "It's just so amazing here."

Some replied with a series of thumbs-up emojis.

One sent a heart emoji.

I thought, *They don't really get it. Should I send a video?*

But then I remembered my own yawns when people share pictures and videos with me. You just can't capture awe with a JPEG file and a caption. Some types of glory aren't meant to be experienced on a screen or a picture.

What's the most indescribable thing you've experienced?

- A physical location, trip, or view?

- The first cry of your newborn child?

- An unexpected check or financial blessing?

- The moment you stood at the altar with your soon-to-be spouse?

- That phone call that made you drop to your knees in relief?

- The sound of your parents reconciling after thirty years of silence?

- The finish line on a race you thought might kill you?

Moments like these are bigger than words. If you're with friends and try to tell them about such a moment, you might wave your hands, smile wide, and speak with so much emotion that your voice eventually breaks. After you've dug as deeply as words can go, your eyes have to tell the rest of the story.

Some moments are meant to be carried, not just told.

Now imagine being the apostle Paul. You've seen the risen Christ. His presence physically blinded you for three days. A stranger's hands touched your head, and your eyes miraculously opened. You've been taken up into visions and revelations. You've watched the dead live again, the sick be healed, prison bars swing open, cities shake, and the gospel set entire families free.

And then the Spirit moves you to write a letter. Physically, you're in a prison cell, but, spiritually, you're somewhere infinitely different. The letter is to spiritually immature church members who not only lack your words but also cannot begin to tap into what you're experiencing.

The Spirit of God speaks: "In Christ, all the fullness of the Deity lives in bodily form, and in Christ you have been brought to fullness" (Colossians 2:9–10).

What do you even do with that?

Or this one: "We will come to them and make our home with them" (John 14:23).

Or: "The Spirit who raised Jesus from the dead is living in you" (Romans 8:11).

How do you explain that the living God, He who is eternal, without end or beginning, Creator of galaxies, Sustainer of history, Source of all knowledge and wisdom, and Redeemer of humanity, now dwells in you?

How do you capture the moment heaven moved in?

This is what I call the *Total Gift Package*. The truth is, most believers have no clue what's sitting in the soil of their heart. We say things like:

- "I got saved."

- "I gave my life to Christ."

- "I received the Spirit."

But those phrases are like calling the Grand Canyon "big."

The New Testament writers wrote exactly what the Spirit gave them. They reached for every metaphor and analogy, such as temple, seed, river, fire, wind, treasure, seal. Yet language falls short because spiritual things are designed to be so much bigger.

Still, the Gift is real. The Spirit is planted in you.

He dwells in you.

He is the fullness of God in you.

The Gift is personal.

Waiting to be known.

Waiting to be fanned into flame.

THE GIFT OF THE DESERT

Let me introduce you to another tree that will impact how you understand what God deposited in you at salvation. The acacia tree is known as "the gift of the desert." If you walked up to one during a drought season, you'd probably think it was dead. No leaves, no visible life, just what looks like weathered wood standing in cracked earth. But you'd be wrong.

That tree isn't dead.

It's dormant.

The acacia tree can stay alive for months and even many years with no rain at all. How? Deep roots. The acacia tree's roots reach all the way down to hidden underground water sources, sometimes extending more than 100 feet below the surface. It taps into reserves most plants can't access, allowing it to survive drought when everything else around it withers and dies.

Acacia wood is one of the strongest hardwoods with the longest burn. When you need fire that lasts, you use acacia. When you need construction material that endures, you use acacia. It's a desert tree designed for endurance and holy purpose. So when God instructed the people of Israel to build the Ark of the Covenant, the vessel that would carry His manifest presence, it's no surprise He chose acacia wood for

- the ark itself (Exodus 25:10).

- the poles for carrying the Ark (Exodus 25:13).

- the table of showbread (Exodus 25:23).

- the poles for the table (Exodus 25:28).

- the frames for the tabernacle (Exodus 26:15–29).

- the altar of burnt offering (Exodus 27:1).

- the poles for the altar (Exodus 27:6).

- the altar of incense (Exodus 30:1).

- the poles for the altar of incense (Exodus 30:5).

The acacia tree represents you. Like every believer, it has been set apart by grace, shaped for holy purposes, and destined to carry God's presence. It holds eternal value even when dormant. You may look dormant to others. You may feel spiritually dry. But there's more in you than anyone can see from the outside, including yourself.

FULL FROM THE START

Back in Chapter 1, I made the case that many believers are either "Word-rich but rain-starved" or "soaked but seedless." That was about diagnosing what's missing. But here in Chapter 3, I want to be clear that when I say, "the seed is there," I'm referring to the fullness of the Holy Spirit at salvation. It's the total supernatural gift package of Himself, salvation, grace, calling, gifts, and the fullness of Him who fills everything in every way.

It's all there.

What may be missing is *formation, discovery, personal revelation, knowledge, and activation.* You may not yet know the Scriptures. You may not have internalized the way of Jesus. But the Spirit is present, and the Spirit brings gifts.

Think of it this way: The seed is in the soil, *and* the soil still needs cultivation. The Spirit has come, *and* the mind must be renewed. This is where Word and Spirit must work together.

What Part of You Is Full?

When you were born again, your spirit wasn't repaired or upgraded. It was made new. Paul writes, "In Christ you have been brought to fullness" (Colossians 2:10). That fullness, the hope of glory, is already in your spirit. That's the part of you that has been raised with Christ, seated in heavenly places, sealed by the Holy Spirit.

Nothing is missing there.

Consider the word *enthusiasm.* It comes from the Latin *entheos,* meaning 'in God'. At its root, enthusiasm is not hype, personality, or emotional energy. It is the overflow that comes from being oriented toward God as the highest and most perfect aim of life. True enthusiasm is not something you manufacture. It emerges when your life is aligned *in Him.* And that "Him" is Jesus.

Now let's be honest. Even if your spirit is full, your emotions may not always feel enthusiastic. You may feel unstable, discouraged, or worn down at times. That doesn't mean the gift has left. It simply means the fullness that is real in your spirit has not yet fully flowed into your soul.

Your thought life may still be contaminated. Your habits may not look like Jesus yet. While salvation is instantaneous in your spirit, sanctification is the ongoing transfer of that fullness into your soul and body over time.

You are a spirit. You have a soul. You live in a body. Scripture sometimes overlaps these words, which can make them difficult to distinguish. Hebrews 4:12 tells us that *the word of God is alive and active,… dividing soul and spirit.*" They are deeply connected, but they are not the same.

Your soul is where your mind, will, emotions, and personality operate. This is where most believers get stuck. They are told, "You're full. You're free. You're gifted," yet their lived experience doesn't seem to line up. Why? Because the Spirit's fullness has not yet superbloomed in their soul.

This is the heart of what it means to live a Spirit-filled life. It's not about chasing goosebumps or emotional highs. It's not even about operating flawlessly in every spiritual gift. When Paul writes to the believers in Corinth, he tells them, *"You do not lack any spiritual gift as you eagerly wait for our Lord Jesus Christ to be revealed"* (1 Corinthians 1:7). Yet only two chapters later he corrects them, saying, *"You are still not ready. You are still worldly"* (1 Corinthians 3:2–3, italics added).

They had the gifts. What they lacked was maturity.

Sanctification is allowing what Christ has already accomplished in your spirit to reshape your thoughts, your desires, your words, and your responses. This is where growth happens. This is where formation takes place. And this is where the superbloom begins to break through the surface.

A personal superbloom occurs when the water of the Spirit in your spirit meets the seed of the Word in your soul. From that union, fruit begins to form:

- fruit of the Spirit

- mature ministry of the gifts of the Spirit

- boldness and power of the Spirit

- wisdom and insight from the Spirit.

None of this grows from the outside in. It grows from the inside out.

So yes, if you are in Christ, you already have the full gift package. Nothing is missing. The gifts are real, and they are present in your spirit. They still need to be activated in your soul and expressed through your life.

Don't be discouraged if you don't feel full yet.

The fullness is real. And when you begin allowing that fullness to flow into every part of who you are, everything starts to change.

THREE "TOTAL GIFT PACKAGE" QUESTIONS

As we dive deeper into what it means to experience the Holy Spirit's activation in your life, I want to address three crucial questions that will determine whether you experience a superbloom or remain dormant.

Question 1: What Is God's Part?

Answer: Everything.

I'm not sure why this even has to be a question. But somewhere along the way, we started treating salvation like a cooperative effort between God's part and our part. His gospel plus our baptism. His grace plus our confession or repentance. His mercy followed by our good behavior. As if we brought something to the table. As if our little moment of faith or quality of our will completed the process.

It's kind of like building a swing set with a toddler. As the parent, you do all the measuring, cutting, bracing, and drilling. Then, right before you finish, you let your son tap in the last nail. Or you wrap his fingers around yours and pull the drill trigger for one final screw. He runs inside, eyes wide and chest puffed out, yelling, "I built the swing set! I built it by myself!"

And you smile because he did help. But also, he didn't.

That's what it's like when we say, "I got saved," as if we were the ones who initiated it. We heard and believed a small part of a much bigger story, one God had been writing for us all along.

Salvation is not something we build. It's something we receive. From the first moment of conviction to the final breath of surrender, it's all grace. All God. He gave us not just forgiveness and not just a new beginning. He gave us Himself. Fully. Entirely.

Yes, God let your will participate through conviction, repentance, and obedience, but even those things were empowered by His Spirit, not your independent good choice to earn His Spirit. Consequently, you didn't get a small deposit of the Holy Spirit. You got the fullness of the Spirit.

It's a mistake to say the gift of the Spirit is "just the indwelling." The gift is His power, presence, grace, fullness, cleansing, renewal, creativity.

The gift is Himself. He's everything.

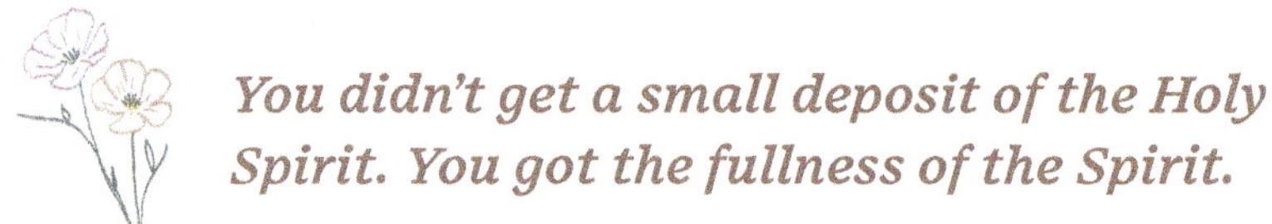

You didn't get a small deposit of the Holy Spirit. You got the fullness of the Spirit.

Paul writes, "When you believed, you were marked in him with a seal, the promised Holy Spirit, who is a deposit guaranteeing our inheritance" (Ephesians 1:13–14). That's not a guarantee of a greater portion of the Spirit at a later time; that's a guarantee of your eternal inheritance of resurrection and eternal life in Christ.

In Titus 3:5–6, the apostle explains that God "saved us through the washing of rebirth and renewal by the Holy Spirit, whom he poured out on us generously through Jesus Christ our Savior." And in Romans 8:9–11, Paul makes it very clear:

> If anyone does not have the Spirit of Christ, they do not belong to Christ. But if Christ is in you, then even though your body is subject to death because of sin, the Spirit gives life because of righteousness. And if the Spirit of him who raised Jesus from the dead is living in you, he who raised Christ from the dead will also give life to your mortal bodies because of his Spirit who lives in you.

The very moment you were born again, the total gift package was placed inside of you. You were sealed. Washed. Reborn. Made alive. Filled. You received

- a new heart of flesh, not stone (Ezekiel 36:26).

- a new mind, the mind of Christ (1 Corinthians 2:16).

- a new spirit, born again (John 3:6–7).

- a new identity, child of God (John 1:12).

- a new power source, the omnipotent Holy Spirit (Acts 1:8).

- a new inheritance, the kingdom of heaven (Matthew 25:34).

You get all of it, all at once.

Here's an example of a believer receiving the total gift package all at once. Notice how Peter uses the language of "the gift" and "baptized with the Holy Spirit" interchangeably:

> As I began to speak, the Holy Spirit came on them as he had come on us at the beginning. Then I remembered what the Lord had said: "John baptized with water, but you will be baptized with the Holy Spirit." So if God gave them the same gift he gave us who believed in the Lord Jesus Christ, who was I to think that I could stand in God's way? (Acts 11:15–16)

Do you see it?

It's like DNA at conception. The fullness is there, *and* the capacity for growth is there too. It may take time to mature, but nothing is missing. When Paul told Timothy to "fan into flame the gift of God, which is in you" (2 Timothy 1:6), he wasn't telling him to go out and get something he didn't already have. The apostle was urging him to stir up what had already been planted.

Whether it refers to salvation, spiritual calling, the Holy Spirit, or all three, "the gift" is something God had already given. Timothy didn't need more of God. He needed greater awareness and activation of what God had already placed within him.

Activation is the key word that is so often misunderstood. Many believers walk around thinking they only received a small portion of the Spirit at salvation. It's like they're waiting on a second blessing or a future baptism to finally "get it all."

But that's not the message of the New Testament. You don't need to get more of the Spirit. You need to realize what's already available. You need the Spirit and His work activated in and through you. You need to stir what's been lying dormant. You need to fan it into flame.

Question 2: What Is Others' Part?

"But what about the laying on of hands?" "What about impartation?" Great questions! I used to say, "I received the baptism of the Holy Spirit in 2005 when so-and-so laid hands on me at the end of a conference." Even today, I'm perfectly okay with people using language like that. If someone says, "I know that I experienced a greater filling of the Spirit when Pastor Eddie laid his hands on me and prophesied over me." I get it. I still use that language when I'm speaking with my various groups of my friends because it's the way they articulate various experiences they've had. I don't push the debate.

However, the more I've studied Scripture and been in anointing, impartation, and Spirit-baptism environments, the more I've realized these are *not* moments where believers receive more of the Holy Spirit or get something new in them. A person touching them or prophesying over them doesn't transmit a gift that wasn't already present and accessible inside them. I'm open to learn more, but this is my most sincere understanding today.

I'm convinced that the moments many call "Spirit baptism" would be better described as **activations** of the anointing or gifts already available by the Spirit in them.

Laying On of Hands, Baptism, and Activation

Some denominations teach a "Second Blessing" theology that someone can be saved but not yet baptized in the Holy Spirit. I understand the heart behind that teaching. They long for people to move in power. They've seen lives transformed when someone gets prayer, speaks in tongues, or suddenly walks in boldness. But I believe there's a more accurate and helpful way to say it.

Rather than, "They haven't received the baptism," I'd say, "They are saved but haven't learned how to walk in the fullness of the Spirit and activate the gifts inside them yet." That shift may seem slight, but it matters. It actually matches the pattern of Scripture.

The Spirit isn't something we have to chase down. He came to live inside us at salvation (see 1 Corinthians 12:13). But just because the Spirit is in you doesn't mean you've been taught how to recognize His voice, drink fully, or operate in His gifts.

That's why Hebrews 6:1–2 lists "laying on of hands" and "baptisms" as elementary teachings, not advanced ones. And it's why moments of prayer, commissioning, prophecy, and community matter deeply. They don't give us something we lack. They awaken what we've already received.

MOSES & JOSHUA

God told Moses to appoint Joshua as the next leader of Israel:

> Take Joshua the son of Nun, **a man in whom is the Spirit**, and lay your hand on him. Make him stand before Eleazar the priest and

all the congregation, and you shall commission him in their sight. (Numbers 27:18–19 ESV, bold added)

Later, we see that Moses obeyed this command, completing the transfer of leadership:

Joshua the son of Nun was full of the spirit of wisdom, for Moses had laid his hands on him. So the people of Israel obeyed him and did as the Lord had commanded Moses. (Deuteronomy 34:9 ESV)

Did Moses transfer wisdom? Or did God use Moses to activate and confirm what was already inside Joshua? The Spirit appears to be already in Joshua and activated by Moses' laying on of hands. Either way, this impartation was a partnership.

No one goes around carrying power in their pockets, but God delights in using His people to activate the fullness of His gifts in others. This divine activation is good news because it means the Spirit of God isn't something you have to chase down from a preacher or seek out at a conference. He's already living in you. The gifts are already His, and He lives in you. The wisdom is already there in Him. The power is already present in Him.

Sometimes all it takes is someone to lay hands on you, pray in faith, speak prophetically, or call you out by name, and what was dormant suddenly erupts into motion. That person didn't give you anything; God used them to activate what He already put in you. I've had hundreds of these moments in my life.

- My aunt laid hands on me when I was thirteen years old and said, "Jeffery, the Lord has gifted you to preach. You're gonna preach."

- My seminary professors laid hands on me and commissioned me to preach the gospel.

- My church elders laid hands on me, and I went to preach full time.

- A man laid hands on me, and I prayed in the Spirit (not for the first time but for the first time that I didn't mock it).

- A man laid hands on me in 2020 and prophesied that I would be involved in governmental areas of ministry in the nation. Four years later, I had three members of the President's Cabinet and others involved in Congress and committees at Anchor Church.

- A man prophesied that it was time to write books and preach the gospel through multiple channels. That activated the writing of this very book.

I care about this deeply. As spiritual leaders, we need to keep maturing in the way we minister in these areas. We need to equip these precious saints in the development of the fullness God has for them and not reduce it all to a sensational experience. At the same time, we do not need to be afraid of sensational experiences. May the Spirit manifest His power, glory, and gifts as He wills, and may we do everything we can to welcome Him.

I love the blessing of prophecy, the laying on of hands, speaking life over others, and helping awaken what God is doing in someone. It's beautiful and sacred. Paul modeled this dynamic when he wrote to Timothy to remind him of what was already there: "Do not neglect your gift, which was given you through prophecy when the body of elders laid their hands on you" (1 Timothy 4:14).

The Greek phrase *edothē soi dia prophēteias* points to the timing and context in which the gift was recognized, not the origin of the gift. The gift seems directly tied to what Paul had just mentioned in verse

13: "Devote yourself to the public reading of Scripture, to preaching and to teaching." The prophecy wasn't the source of the gift; it was the setting in which it was activated, affirmed, or identified. Likewise, the laying on of hands (*meta epitheseōs tōn cheirōn*) was a common biblical practice for commissioning, confirming, and blessing (not for transferring divine power). Think of it as a holy moment of alignment, not a supernatural transaction.

Some might argue, "Well, God gave Timothy the gift, but Paul was the conduit, and prophecy was the vehicle God used to place the gift inside Timothy." I understand that line of thinking, but I don't think it's necessary to see it that way. In 2 Timothy 1:6, Paul writes, "Fan into flame the gift of God, which is in you through the laying on of my hands." The Greek phrase *dia tēs epitheseōs tōn cheirōn* emphasizes means or setting, not origin. Paul is saying, in effect, "You have this gift—it's in you. I was there when it was affirmed. Now stir it up."

The laying on of hands wasn't the moment the Spirit entered Timothy; it was the moment the fire got fanned. The gifts are distributed by the Spirit as He wills (1 Corinthians 12:11), and every believer has already been blessed with "every spiritual blessing in Christ" (Ephesians 1:3).

So yes, God placed the total gift package in you at salvation. Others may affirm it, help stir it up, and even lay hands in agreement, but they don't create it. They help wake it up. That's why spiritual community matters. You need people to recognize, confirm, and call out what God has already planted in you.

- "I see the gift of teaching when you explain Scripture."

- "I see a pastoral heart when you care for people in crisis."

- "I see prophetic insight when you pray with boldness and clarity."

- "I see the grace of God at work through your generosity."

Remember, the acacia tree was chosen for the Ark of the Covenant, the altar, the table of showbread, and all the carrying poles. It was a tree set apart for sacred purposes.

That's you. You're not just a human being. You're a vessel set apart for God's presence, a carrier of His glory. But you need spiritual family to help you see it. You need others to confirm and awaken what God has already put inside you.

Question 3: What Is My Part?

Every athlete knows the difference between what the coaches will do, what the fans can do, and what they must do. Trainers can create the meal plans, calculate the supplement regimen, and plaster motivational sayings all over the weight room. But the athlete is the one who actually has to commit to those routines and disciplines.

When I teach people Scripture and they surrender to Christ by faith, they become new believers. I can prophesy over them, lay my hands on them, and speak life into them. I can declare God's Word over them and tell them all that now resides within them. I can enroll them in a discipleship path that teaches them the Word, the ways of Christ, the disciplines of the Spirit, and everything I've learned about maturity.

But they still have to do their part. This third question is the key to activating what's inside you. It's also the part many people resist. There's no shortcut. No one can read or memorize the Word for you. No one can agree with the Word and Spirit for you. No one can open your mouth and pray for you.

Paul says, "Fan into flame the gift." Some translations say, "Stir up the gift" (NKJV, KJV). Both verbs indicate action. You cannot passively fan or stir something and expect meaningful results.

Let me use an analogy from my own life. Recently, my son wanted to learn how to grill chicken. I lit up the charcoal and started walking him through the process. "You've got to keep that vent open in the back," I told him. "If air doesn't get through, the fire won't last." How does grilling connect to spiritual superbloom?

Water is to seed what wind is to hot coals.

When a fire is dormant, just a little air breathed onto glowing coals can activate a flame.

Water activates dormant seeds in the desert. Wind activates dormant coals in the fire. Both require the right conditions *and* intentional application.

Fresh Wind = Praying in the Holy Spirit

In Ephesians 6:18, Paul instructs, "And pray in the Spirit on all occasions with all kinds of prayers and requests." *Always* pray in the Spirit. Never stop praying in the Spirit. Keep the vent on your heart open at all times, not just mealtime or bedtime prayers. That means having an ongoing, relational, Spirit-led, Spirit-moved, Spirit-motivated, Spirit-empowered conversation with God. This is the most effective way to stir dormant faith and reawaken spiritual gifts.

Hot Coals = Bold Prayers

Bold prayers are those where you think, *If I pray this, something's going to change,* or even, *If I pray this, I might have to start something I said I'd never do.* When your natural mind stops agreeing with the enemy's limitations and your spirit starts agreeing with God's possibilities, fire ignites.

Your city needs bold prayers. Your family needs bold prayers. Your calling needs bold prayers.

Fresh Wood = Radical Obedience

There's no point praying bold prayers if you won't obey what He says. If you pray, "God, You say it, and I'll do it. Tell me, and I'll obey," then do it. Just one day. Then tell me what happens. That's how you bring fresh wood onto the fire of God in your heart.

Fresh wood is a living word, a quickened command, or leading of the Spirit in full alignment with Scripture. When this happens in prayer, something comes alive in your entire being. You're walking in the Spirit. You're activating faith by receiving the Word and putting it into practice. Jesus said that when you live this way, you're like a wise person building their life on a solid foundation. But if you ignore this, you're building on sand.

When you pray in the Spirit, the vent stays open. You'll sense His presence and voice in every conversation, every decision, and every place you go. You'll get downloads of wisdom, revelation, encouragement, and power all throughout the day. The flesh will lose its grip. Negative news might pass through your thoughts, but it won't have any power to stick.

THE FULL MEASURE ALREADY LIVES IN YOU

> For while we are in this tent, we groan and are burdened, because we do not wish to be unclothed but to be clothed instead with our heavenly dwelling, so that what is mortal may be swallowed up by life. Now the one who has fashioned us for this very purpose is

God, who has given us the Spirit as a deposit, guaranteeing what is to come. (2 Corinthians 5:4–5)

God saved you to glorify you. He already sees you seated with Him in eternity. You're already raised in His eternal view. You're already filled, right now. When you pray in the Spirit, when you contend in faith, you're tasting heaven. That's what's supposed to happen.

This isn't about charismatic vs. cessationist theology. It's about a Spirit-filled, blood-bought Church coming alive in the gifts and presence of God. The real God lives in you. And when superbloom hits, the first thing to change won't be your circumstances. It will be you.

The Apostle's Hunger

Paul wrote to the believers in Rome, "I long to see you so that I may impart to you some spiritual gift to make you strong—that is, that you and I may be mutually encouraged by each other's faith" (Romans 1:11–12). The apostle wasn't saying, "I'm bringing something you don't have" but "I want to activate what is in you so we can both be greatly encouraged." What was in them needed to be activated. That's spiritual community. That's mutual impartation. That's divine grit, as both people come alive more fully in hard places, through disciplined, God-centered lives.

What About Timothy?

Timothy likely became the greatest church multiplier in the New Testament, pastoring in Ephesus and eventually helping lead the entire province of Asia. Yet in Revelation 2:4, the Spirit says to that very church, "I hold this against you: You have forsaken the love you had at first." Even Timothy, with all his heritage, mentoring, gifts, and calling, needed a reminder that fanning into flame isn't a one-time event. It's a lifestyle.

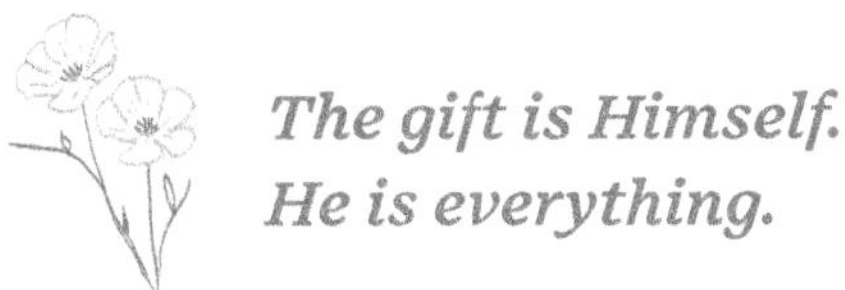

The gift is Himself.
He is everything.

Back to Your First Love

Imagine if you went back to your first love and said, "Lord, take me back to the kindergarten of discovering what's in me. Help me grow up in You. Activate everything You've put inside of me." What might happen?

Jude 20–21 gives us the roadmap:

> But you, dear friends, by building yourselves up in your most holy faith and praying in the Holy Spirit, keep yourselves in God's love as you wait for the mercy of our Lord Jesus Christ to bring you to eternal life.

Build yourself up. Pray in the Spirit. Stay in God's love. That's how you fan into flame the gift of God within you.

The superbloom rises from within. And when it does, you won't just attend church. You'll carry the kingdom. Your prayers will shift atmospheres. Your faith will carry and release the impossible. The total gift package is yours. It has been and will be.

CHAPTER 3 STUDY GUIDE

Now the one who has fashioned us for this very purpose is God, who has given us the Spirit as a deposit, guaranteeing what is to come.

—2 Corinthians 5:5

REVIEW

Every believer receives access to God's full presence and power at salvation. This total gift package includes grace, calling, spiritual gifts, and the indwelling of the Holy Spirit. Like the acacia tree in the desert, there may be times when we appear dry or dormant, but unseen roots still draw from the living water of God's Spirit. What looks lifeless is often just waiting for activation.

Your spirit was made completely new when you were born again, but your soul and body must align with that reality. Sanctification is the ongoing process of allowing what God has already placed in your spirit to reshape your thoughts, desires, and actions.

Three crucial questions arise: *What is God's part? What is others' part? What is my part?* While salvation is entirely God's work, spiritual community activates what He has already given. Your role is to "fan into flame" the gift of God through prayer in the Spirit, bold faith, and radical obedience.

The Word and the Spirit work together to produce transformation. You already carry everything needed for a supernatural life. The superbloom begins when what God has already planted in you awakens through faith and surrender.

KEY SCRIPTURES

In Christ, all the fullness of the Deity lives in bodily form, and in Christ you have been brought to fullness. (Colossians 2:9–10)

If anyone does not have the Spirit of Christ, they do not belong to Christ. But if Christ is in you, then even though your body is subject to death because of sin, the Spirit gives life because of righteousness. And if the Spirit of him who raised Jesus from the dead is living in you, he who raised Christ from the dead will also give life to your mortal bodies because of his Spirit who lives in you. (Romans 8:9–11)

Fan into flame the gift of God, which is in you. (2 Timothy 1:6)

When you believed, you were marked in him with a seal, the promised Holy Spirit, who is a deposit guaranteeing our inheritance. (Ephesians 1:13–14)

GROUP DISCUSSION

1. How might common Christian language actually minimize our understanding of what happens at salvation? How can we better communicate the magnitude of the total gift package?

2. What does the acacia tree's ability to survive drought reveal about believers in spiritually dry seasons?

3. Why is community essential for recognizing and calling out gifts? How can we develop environments that promote healthy activation and deter unhealthy spiritual dependence?

4. What safeguards keep the "laying on of hands" from becoming transactional or celebrity-driven?

5. If the body of Christ truly understood the fullness deposited at salvation, what changes would you expect to see in church culture, personal spiritual life, and Kingdom impact?

PERSONAL REFLECTION

1. During spiritually dry seasons in your life, how does knowing you have deep roots in Christ influence your perspective on what appears dormant versus what is actually available

2. How does understanding that salvation is entirely God's work affect your confidence in the total gift package?

3. Who in your life has helped you recognize what God already planted in you? How can you serve as part of a spiritual community for others?

4. Your part in activation involves fresh wind (praying in the Spirit), hot coals (bold prayers), and fresh wood (radical obedience). Which of these three areas represents your greatest opportunity for growth? What specific changes would strengthen your ability to "fan into flame" what God has given you?

PRAYER

Father God, thank You for the total gift package You placed inside me at salvation. Open my eyes to see the fullness of Your Spirit already dwelling in me. Please surround me with a strong spiritual community of people who will recognize, confirm, and call out what You've planted in me. Make me that person for others as well. Teach me to fan into flame the gifts You've given me. May fresh wind through praying in the Spirit, hot coals through bold prayers, and fresh wood through radical obedience activate what lies dormant. Let sanctification flow from my spirit into my soul and body until the superbloom rises from within for Your glory. In Jesus' name, Amen.

4

UNDER THE INFLUENCE

When you strip it of everything else, Pentecost stands for power and life. That's what came into the church when the Holy Spirit came down on the day of Pentecost.

—**David Wilkerson,** *The Cross and the Switchblade*

I will sprinkle clean water on you … I will give you a new heart and put a new spirit in you.

—**Ezekiel 36:25–26**

I HAD MY first taste of beer when I was about nine years old. We were at a relative's house in South Louisiana, and a few of the older men were drinking and laughing. I asked one of them, "What's that?"

"It's good. Try it," he said, grinning. My eyes lit up. I picked up the can with both hands like it was treasure. But the moment I smelled it, I knew it was a trap.

"Go ahead! It's good," another one chimed in. I shifted from cautious to brave and took a sip.

The second it hit my mouth, I spit it out with a dramatic, "Bluuuhaaakkkchhhh. Ugh!" They all burst into laughter. If it had tasted like orange Kool-Aid, we'd have been in trouble. But it did not.

That moment pretty much sealed it for me. Through all my teenage years, I never touched alcohol. In college, I might've had five drinks total (usually at weddings) but never more than a sip or two. I just didn't like the taste.

I've never been drunk. I've never even been buzzed on purpose. But there was one time I accidentally got "filled" with the wrong spirit. It was 2015, just before the launch of Anchor Church, and Bill Beck, one of our core team members, was turning fifty. My wife, Sarah, and I went to his party. About two hours in, I was holding court in the kitchen when Sarah walked up beside me and whispered, "I didn't know you liked vodka."

I replied, "I don't."

"Well, you're drinking it."

"No, I'm not," I countered. "I'm drinking that punch."

"Which one?"

I pointed to the glass container on the right. "The one that says, 'For Kids.'"

Sarah raised an eyebrow. "The sign points to the left. The one you're drinking has vodka in it. How many have you had?"

I blurted out, "Six!"

She grinned. "I knew something was off. You're talking loud … and a lot."

For the next thirty minutes, I became the life of the party. I told everyone I could about my accidental dive into the world of mixed drinks.

The next morning, one verse hit me like never before: "Do not get drunk on wine, which leads to debauchery. Instead, be filled with the Spirit" (Ephesians 5:18). Suddenly, it made sense. Even with just an accidental buzz, things had shifted. My judgment, my character, and my talk were impacted by that seemingly innocent punch. It made me wonder what happens when the Spirit of God fills a person like that. Not in a goofy, overhyped way but in a deeply transformative, unmistakable way.

As we continue this Superbloom journey, I want to explore this question: *What are the signs that someone is truly under the influence of the Spirit?* That's a more helpful question than "Who has the baptism?" What good is it to claim an experience if you don't have a lifestyle of drinking deeply from the Spirit, walking in fellowship with Him, and operating in His anointing?

The Spirit changes everything from the inside out. And those changes will always show up in three places:

- Your power (judgment, discernment, anointing);

- Your walk (ministry, purpose, lifestyle); and

- Your talk (speech, worship, praise, prayer).

These are the signs of a life not only touched by God but also filled and fueled by Him.

THREE SIGNS YOU'RE UNDER THE INFLUENCE

Two foundational Scriptures frame this whole chapter:

> We were all baptized by one Spirit so as to form one body ... and we were all given the one Spirit to drink. (1 Corinthians 12:13)

> Do not get drunk on wine ... instead, be filled with the Spirit. (Ephesians 5:18)

Note that in this second verse, "filled" in Greek is the present passive imperative. It literally means 'keep on being filled.' You were meant to be initially filled, and you were meant to keep drinking. To keep walking. To stay under the influence of the Spirit every day.

Let's explore the signs that you're doing just that.

Sign #1: Your Power Changes

When you drink alcohol, the first part of your brain to be affected is the prefrontal cortex, the area responsible for judgment, self-awareness, moral reasoning, and decision-making. The first thing to go? Clarity. You start to lose your sense of power. You can't process courage realistically, discern risk accurately, or think clearly about what matters most.

But when you drink of the Spirit, you gain real, supernatural power. Paul reminds Timothy in 2 Timothy 1:7, "God has not given us a spirit of fear and timidity, but of power, love, and self-discipline" (NLT). That word power is *dynamis*, and it's the same miraculous, divine power often used to describe the work of the Holy Spirit in the New Testament.

How Your Power Changes with the Spirit

1. Supernatural Courage

They were all filled with the Holy Spirit and spoke the word of God boldly. (Acts 4:31)

When you're under the Spirit's influence, fear loses its grip. Instead of shrinking back, you step forward. You endure.

2. Spiritual Authority

I have given you authority … to overcome all the power of the
enemy. (Luke 10:19)

I've spent too much of my life seeking approval. I'm still working on
that, but I've learned that authority doesn't come from affirmation. It
comes from the Spirit. When you're filled with His power, you stop
needing everyone else's permission to be who God called you to be.
Drink of the Spirit, and you'll walk in spiritual authority every time.

3. Miraculous Ability

You will receive power when the Holy Spirit comes on you.
(Acts 1:8)

That power isn't just for Pentecost. It's for you too. If you've been
taught that the Spirit no longer works miracles, I'd lovingly ask you
to reconsider. The same Spirit that raised Jesus is alive in you, and He
hasn't retired.

4. Endurance for Difficult Assignments

Being strengthened with all power according to his glorious might
so that you may have great endurance and patience.
(Colossians 1:11)

There have been many times I didn't think I'd make it in ministry.
I've experienced fear, fatigue, doubt, and anxiety. But every time, the
Spirit has met me in that moment and filled me again with strength
to keep going. That's not adrenaline or willpower. That's Spirit-filled
perseverance.

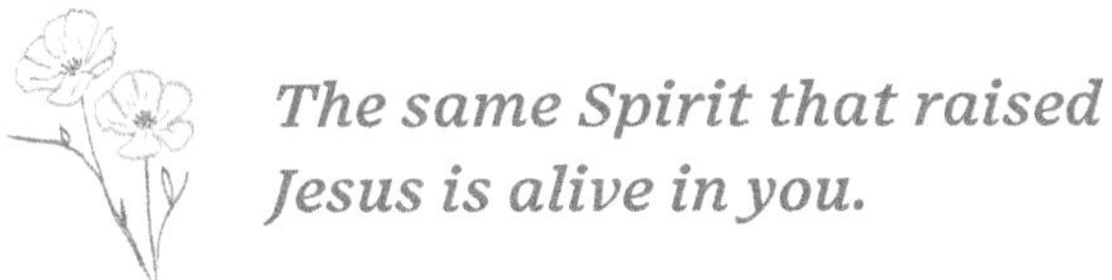

*The same Spirit that raised
Jesus is alive in you.*

5. Divine Discernment

> Very truly I tell you, the Son can do nothing by himself; he can do only what he sees his Father doing, because whatever the Father does the Son also does. (John 5:19)

When Jesus received the Holy Spirit at His baptism, He didn't operate out of emotion or insecurity. He moved in rhythm with the Father. When Paul was under the influence of legalism, he arrested Christians. But when he was filled with the Spirit, everything about him changed.

I remember when my son, Hayden, was being recruited by LSU. He'd been to Tiger Stadium before, but this was different. This time, he wasn't just a spectator. He had a lanyard with his name on it. Coaches were talking to him. That shift from spectator to participant changes your whole state of mind. You walk differently. You talk differently. You feel like you could fight a bear with a stick.

When you're under the influence of the Spirit, you walk into rooms differently. It's not because you're trying to impress people with your words but because His power is working through you. In Acts 16, Paul and Silas weren't complaining in prison; they were worshipping. Their worship changed the atmosphere. And then God changed the environment.

The Lord paid too high a price for us to walk in weak power. Say this out loud: "There's more in here." More in your home. More in your ministry. More in your spirit. Why? Because He's in you.

So why don't more people walk in this kind of power? Because we're drinking other stuff.

5 Things That Drain Your Spiritual Power

1. **The Religious Sippy Cup**—Surface-level sermons and Sunday checklists are spiritual pacifiers. If you're not praying, worshipping, or fellowshipping with the Spirit, then you're spiritually dehydrated.

2. **The Social Media Funnel**—You're drinking in comparison, shame, and inadequacy through your eyes all day long. No wonder you feel discouraged.

3. **Regret Whiskey Glasses**—Constantly replaying past mistakes keeps you drunk on remorse and numb to hope.

4. **Shots of Bitterness**—A single bitter moment can poison your whole year and your whole soul. Bitter shots deepen bitter roots.

5. **The Perfection Pitcher**—If you're clinging to religious performance out of fear of imperfection, you're rejecting the grace that sets you free.

Access to the Spirit of power is available, but it requires some intentionality to stop drinking in ways that drain your power.

Sign #2: Your Walk Changes

The cerebellum is the part of your brain that controls coordination and movement, including how you walk. That's why intoxicated people stumble. Even if they don't feel drunk, their bodies show it.

In the same way, when the Spirit fills you, your walk starts to mirror His. In ancient Judaism, to follow a rabbi meant to walk so closely behind him that you'd be covered in his dust. As someone's disciple, you literally walked the way he walked, went where he went, and did what he did.

The Spirit affects how you live, move, and respond. When you're under His influence, you start walking differently in five key areas.

1. Your Priorities Shift

What used to matter most doesn't anymore. You find yourself caring more about people than possessions, more about eternity than entertainment.

2. Your Responses Change

Instead of reacting out of hurt or anger, you respond with grace. You don't lose your temper as quickly. You forgive faster.

3. Your Relationships Deepen

You stop trying to impress people and start trying to serve them. You become a safe person whom others can trust with their struggles.

4. Your Risk Tolerance Increases

You step into things that used to terrify you because you know He's with you. You say yes to God even when you don't understand His plan.

5. Your Pace Becomes Sustainable

You stop running on empty and start moving in rhythm with the Spirit. Rest becomes worship, not laziness.

When the Spirit Was Activated in Me

For years, I thought I just needed to "get my act together." But in 2005, I attended a conference where people were being activated in the Spirit, and I realized I needed *more*.

I stayed seated at first, skeptical. I'd prayed in tongues before but decisively doubted it was real. (I'll teach more on that later.) Because of my uncertainty and my desire to stay in control, I didn't expect anything to happen if I did respond.

But then I sensed the Lord whisper, *Jeff, you're afraid of what you can't control. You need more of My love. Trust me. Move.*

So, I did.

I walked to the front.

After about ten minutes of standing with my eyes closed and wholeheartedly seeking the Lord, an older pastor came up to me, put a hand on my chest, and asked, "What do you want, son?"

I said, "I want all that God has for me."

He prayed, "Fill him, Lord."

For the next forty-five minutes, I lay on the front row, praying in the Spirit with all kinds of prayers and several short bursts of weeping in love. This wasn't because I got the "baptism" but because the Spirit in me was activated by faith. The Spirit of love immediately changed my walk.

From that moment on, I never stopped intentionally operating in the gifts of the Spirit and experiencing power in my walk. I no longer believed I "had a gift" and needed to take a spiritual gift test to figure out which one. I immediately knew the Spirit was personally in me to administer whatever gifts or works He willed.

This was a huge shift for me. I'll explain in much more depth later.

Sign #3: Your Talk Changes

Broca's area (frontal lobe) and Wernicke's area (temporal lobe) manage your speech and language production. That's why intoxicated people often slur their words or struggle to form coherent sentences. Rambling and confusion also come from alcohol's effects on the prefrontal cortex and other regions involved in judgment and memory.

Spiritually speaking, the same thing is true. James 3:4 explains how the tongue is like the rudder of the ship. Proverbs 18:21 says, "The tongue has the power of life and death." Ephesians 5:18–19 says being filled with the Spirit leads to "psalms and hymns and spiritual songs, singing and making melody to the Lord with your heart" (ESV).

The Spirit changes your language. We need sound minds and sound speech. We need our words to create peace, not confusion. We need prophecy, not gossip, and praise, not slander. We need truth, not exaggeration. When God fills you with the Spirit, the overflow shows up in your words through your prayers, your encouragement, and your declarations.

HOW DO I DRINK OF THE SPIRIT?

> How much more will your Father in heaven give the Holy Spirit to those who ask Him! (Luke 11:13)

Ask. It really is that simple. And build a lifestyle of drinking deeply.

Here's how I practice it:

1. Enter His Presence Intentionally

Acknowledge God. Welcome Him. Worship Him all day long.

> Let anyone who is thirsty come to me and drink. (John 7:37)

> Enter His gates with thanksgiving,
> and his courts with praise;
> give thanks to him and praise his name. (Psalm 100:4)

2. Receive Mercy and Grace Throughout the Day

The key to fellowship with the Holy Spirit is to keep your repentance list short. Don't let sin stack up. Most people who believe they might lose their salvation are confusing salvation with fellowship with the Spirit. Every time you confess and repent, fellowship with the Spirit flows like a fountain.

> If we confess our sins, he is faithful and just and will forgive us our sins and purify us from all unrighteousness. (1 John 1:9)

3. Receive His Voice Through His Word

The Spirit and the Word are one, and there is no greater way to drink of the Spirit than to receive the Word of God. When you do, it becomes living and active inside you. When you read, ask: "Holy Spirit, what are You saying to me?"

> Man shall not live on bread alone, but on every word that comes from the mouth of God. (Matthew 4:4)

4. Pray in the Spirit

It's less about talking nonstop and more about being present with Him. You can pray on all occasions and without ceasing when you understand that 95 percent of prayer is listening and being present.

> Pray in the Spirit on all occasions with all kinds of prayers and requests. (Ephesians 6:18)

5. Pour Out What He Gives You

The Spirit is an endless river. Drink deeply. Overflow freely. The Superbloom you've been longing for starts when you stop sipping religion and start drinking from the Spirit of the living God.

> Do not merely listen to the word, and so deceive yourselves. Do what it says. (James 1:22)

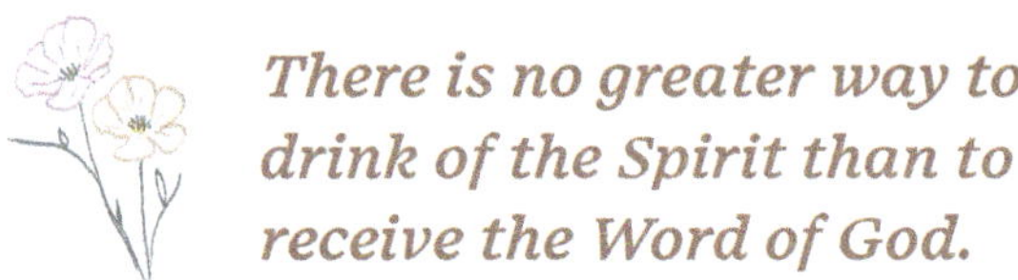

There is no greater way to drink of the Spirit than to receive the Word of God.

Warning: The moment you start drinking deeply from the Spirit, you'll discover there are other forces at work trying to contaminate your soil. Just like a rancher who discovers anthrax has poisoned his land, we must learn to discern what's growing in the garden of our hearts. Not every spiritual experience comes from the right source. In the next chapter, we will look at how to deal with a deadly superbloom.

CHAPTER 4 STUDY GUIDE

Do not get drunk on wine, which leads to debauchery. Instead, be filled with the Spirit.

—Ephesians 5:18

REVIEW

Being "under the influence" of the Holy Spirit means living in continuous dependence on His power. The Greek word for filled in Ephesians 5:18 is the present passive imperative, meaning 'keep on being filled.' This is a lifestyle of drinking from the Spirit, not a single event.

Just as alcohol affects your judgment, coordination, and speech, the Holy Spirit transforms these areas when you're filled with Him. Your power changes as the Spirit gives supernatural courage, spiritual authority, miraculous ability, endurance for difficult assignments, and divine discernment. Your walk changes as priorities shift toward eternal things, responses become grace-filled, relationships deepen, risk tolerance increases, and your pace becomes sustainable as you move in rhythm with Him. Finally, your talk changes as the overflow of the Spirit shows up in your words through prayers instead of complaints, encouragement instead of gossip, and worship instead of grumbling.

If you drink from any other source, your power is drained, and to drink deeply of the Spirit requires intentionality. Enter His presence through worship. Receive mercy and grace by keeping short accounts with God and receive His voice through Scripture. Pray in the Spirit and pour out what He gives you through obedient action.

KEY SCRIPTURES

We were all baptized by one Spirit so as to form one body ... and we were all given the one Spirit to drink. (1 Corinthians 12:13)

God has not given us a spirit of fear and timidity, but of power, love, and self-discipline. (2 Timothy 1:7)

You will receive power when the Holy Spirit comes on you. (Acts 1:8)

How much more will your Father in heaven give the Holy Spirit to those who ask Him! (Luke 11:13)

GROUP DISCUSSION

1. When someone's behavior makes it obvious that they are "under the influence" of a substance, what are the signs? What should be the signs that someone is under the influence of the Spirit?

2. How does the body of Christ sometimes fall into the trap of seeking human validation rather than operating in Spirit-given authority? What would it look like for us to encourage each other toward Spirit-empowered living instead?

3. How can we help each other walk as closely with Jesus today as ancient disciples did with their rabbis?

4. What is the biggest drain on spiritual power in our generation or community? How can we help each other recognize when we're drinking from the wrong sources?

5. How does worship, both corporate and personal, help us
    stay filled with the Spirit? What role should worship and
    verbal praise play in our gatherings and daily lives as a com-
    munity?

PERSONAL REFLECTION

1. Of the three signs (power, walk, talk), which area of your life
    shows the clearest evidence that you're filled with the Spirit?
    Which area needs strengthening?

2. When was the last time you experienced supernatural cour-
    age, spiritual authority, or miraculous ability? What were
    you "drinking" during that season?

3. Which of the five power-draining sources (religious perfor-
    mance, social media, regret, bitterness, perfectionism) do
    you find yourself turning to most often? What would it look
    like to replace that with drinking from the Spirit instead?

4. How will you commit to drinking of the Spirit intentionally
    this week?

PRAYER

*Father God, we want to live under the influence of Your Spirit. We con-
fess that we've tried to walk in our own strength, drinking from sources
that drain rather than sustain us. Please forgive us, Lord. We invite You to
transform our power, our walk, and our talk. Activate our supernatural
courage to speak boldly about the gospel of Jesus Christ and awaken our*

spiritual authority to overcome the enemy. May we operate in divine discernment to see what You're doing and endurance to persevere in difficult times. We surrender our desire for control and ask You to fill us continually. Teach us to drink deeply from You every day. In Jesus' name, Amen.

5

WHAT'S IN THE SOIL?

Resolution One: I will live for God. Resolution Two: If no one else does, I still will.

—Jonathan Edwards

I would rather feel compassion than know the meaning of it. I would hope to act with compassion without thinking of personal gain.

—Thomas Aquinas

WHEN I NEED real time with my son, with no distractions and no noise, I call one of two people: Brad or Andrew. Both of them own ranches and understand the deep need fathers have to connect with their sons in the wild, away from phones, pressures, and the churn of everyday life. They get it. They know that something sacred happens out there.

This time, I called Andrew. It was mid-July 2019. Smothering heat. Hunting season hadn't started yet. But wild hogs? They're always in season. Hayden and I loaded up the truck and drove five hours southwest to High Well Ranch in Sonora, Texas. Andrew's land is no joke. It's 1,000 acres, high-fenced, loaded with whitetail deer, Texas Dall sheep, aoudads, exotic antelope, blackbucks, and more. Normally, the place is alive. You can't drive 100 yards without kicking up a herd of something.

But not this time.

As soon as we arrived, something felt off. No hogs. No deer. No blackbucks skipping across the field near the front blind. Nothing. We sat in the stand for two hours that first evening and didn't see a single animal. On the way back to camp, we noticed something strange: a dead deer on the side of the trail.

Then another. Then another.

By the time we reached the lodge, I'd counted eleven dead deer. I was somewhere between confused, creeped out, and concerned. I texted some photos to Andrew, and within the hour, he called back with the answer.

Anthrax. Apparently, there had been a sudden anthrax outbreak in a 4.2-million-acre territory including Sonora. Nearly every ranch in the area lost its entire population of grass-eating animals. Just like that.

Andrew and I did a little digging. Turns out, anthrax spores can lie dormant in hot, dry, desert-like soil for years and even decades. Nobody sees it. Nobody thinks about it. But one day, a heavy rain hits, and the anthrax spores get activated, affecting everything growing from the soil.

It's a toxic form of superbloom. And it's exactly what happens in the spiritual life too.

There are things buried deep in the soil of our hearts, things we think will never manifest publicly, things we've ignored, or things we never knew were there. They lie dormant until the conditions are just right. Sometimes a storm rolls in. A downpour hits. And what's been hiding in the ground suddenly rises up and starts showing in our lives, work, and relationships.

Sometimes blessing, promotion, or favor with men causes these things to superbloom. If you've ever seen a believer or a leader exposed with a barrage of secret sin, I can almost guarantee you there was a super-bloom-like activation after a period of prosperity.

The good thing is, God gives us time to repent and cleanse the soil of our lives. If we don't, the root spirits will manifest in a destructive end.

PAUL KNEW ABOUT CONTAMINATED SOIL

Before you think I'm taking this metaphor too far, let me show you something. Paul dealt with this exact same issue in Corinth. His solution wasn't to throw out the supernatural but to clean up the soil.

The church in Corinth had everything: tongues, prophecy, healings, miracles, and so on. They were experiencing what looked like a full-blown spiritual superbloom. But Paul looked at their situation and said something shocking: "When you come together it is not for the better but for the worse" (1 Corinthians 11:17 ESV).

People were coming to church, operating in the gifts of the Spirit and seeking to encounter God. But they were leaving more wounded, confused, and messed up than when they arrived. How was that possible?

The gifts were real. The power was real. But the soil was infected. And that contamination was affecting everything growing from it.

Paul's diagnosis wasn't that they needed fewer spiritual experiences. Instead, they needed to become a different kind of people. Before he ever lists a single spiritual gift in 1 Corinthians 12, the apostle uses a crucial word that sets the tone for everything: *pneumatikos*. It doesn't just mean spiritual gifts. It literally means 'spiritual things' or 'things of the Spirit.' But more importantly, it describes the kind of person who can actually handle spiritual things. This person is someone whose life, mind, and decisions are governed by the Spirit rather than the flesh.

In other words, Paul was saying, "Before we talk about the gifts, we need to talk about what kind of soil receives them."

Two Kinds of Soil

In 1 Corinthians 2:14–15, Paul contrasts two types of people.

- The **Psuchikos** person is the natural, soulish, flesh-governed "person without the Spirit [who] does not accept the things that come from the Spirit of God" (v. 14).

- The **Pneumatikos** person is the discerning "person with the Spirit [who] makes judgments about all things" (v. 15).

The Corinthians had the gifts (*charismata*) actively manifesting in their church, but Paul makes it painfully clear: Spiritual gifts were blooming in soil that was still full of flesh, division, pride, and demonic confusion.

Here are the contaminants in the spiritual atmosphere in Corinth:

- Spiritual pride and gift comparison (1 Corinthians 1:12; 12:21–25)

- Sexual immorality tolerated within the church (1 Corinthians 5:1)

- Boasting about grace while tolerating sin (1 Corinthians 5:2)

- Lawsuits among believers (1 Corinthians 6:1–7)

- Chaos in marriage and family roles (1 Corinthians 7)

- Idolatry and divided loyalties (1 Corinthians 8–10)

- Drunkenness and disorder during communion
  (1 Corinthians 11:20–22)

- Tongues without interpretation, causing confusion
  (1 Corinthians 14:9, 23)

- Prophetic words out of order and untested
  (1 Corinthians 14:29)

- A lack of love and maturity beneath the gifts
  (1 Corinthians 13:1–3).

They had a superbloom of gifts, but their soil was infected.

I remember visiting a church a few years ago where the worship was electric, the preaching was powerful, and people were getting healed. But something felt off. During the ministry time, I watched a woman approach the altar for prayer. The moment the pastor laid hands on her, she collapsed and began convulsing. "Depression is leaving!" the pastor shouted. The crowd cheered. But I felt the Holy Spirit whisper, *That's not depression. And it's not leaving.*

This happens a lot. I recognize manipulation, coined phrases, and spiritual jargon that leaders have put in their verbal arsenal over the years. It looks and sounds spiritual, but it's not the Holy Spirit. What I witnessed was a manifestation, not of deliverance but of control. The spirit working through that situation wasn't the Holy Spirit; it was a religious spirit that thrived on dramatic displays and the pastor's need to be seen as someone with spiritual power and authority.

The woman left that night thinking she was free. Two weeks later, she was hospitalized for a severe episode. Real power doesn't need to perform. Real deliverance doesn't need an audience. Real discernment can tell the difference.

That's exactly what Paul was dealing with in Corinth: real gifts operating through contaminated soil.

The Heart of the Problem

Paul's primary concern was that even though the Corinthians had plenty of gifts, they lacked the pure maturity to discern spiritual things and operate from the Spirit. Because their soil was mixed, the manifestations of the Spirit were being distorted by the presence of the flesh and unaddressed root spirits.

So how do we become *pneumatikos*?

The answer is in Hebrews 5:14: "Solid food is for the mature, who by constant use have trained themselves to distinguish good from evil." In the Greek, the word distinguish is also translated as *discern*. Spiritual maturity is more than knowing right from wrong. It's about being able to discern what's in the soil. Not just the visible fruit but the invisible roots too. Not just behaviors but the spiritual forces that animate them.

This is why Paul introduces the gift of "discerning spirits" in 1 Corinthians 12:10. More than casting demons out of people (though that may happen too), it's about exposing what has been tolerated in the soil.

WHEN THE FOG FINALLY LIFTED

Rachel had been struggling for three years, though she'd never told anyone the full extent of it. She loved Jesus. She had for years. She was faithful, generous, and always the one others called when they needed prayer. She served in the children's ministry, led a small group, and rarely missed a Sunday service. From the outside, she looked like the picture of spiritual health.

But inside, something was dying. Rachel couldn't feel anything when she worshipped. Her time in God's Word felt like reading a phone book. She would wake up tired, drag through her day in a spiritual fog, and scroll late into the night to numb the dull ache in her soul. She wasn't in sin, and she wasn't backsliding. She just felt *nothing*.

Rachel's doctor said it was probably depression and offered medication. Her counselor told her it was burnout and suggested a sabbatical. Her friends said it was hormones and would pass with time. But deep down, Rachel knew something else was wrong.

The breakthrough came on a Wednesday night during a prayer gathering. Rachel had almost stayed home, again. But something urged her to go, even though she felt like she was just going through the motions.

During the ministry time in worship, a woman she barely knew, someone who'd been praying quietly in the corner, approached her. "Hi, I'm Linda," she said gently. "I don't really know you, but I feel like the Lord is showing me something. Have you been feeling like you're living under a fog? Like there's something blocking your ability to connect with God?"

Rachel's eyes filled with tears. That was exactly how she'd describe it. "I feel like you're dealing with a spirit of stupor," Linda continued. "Like something has been sent to make you spiritually numb and even drowsy. Can I pray with you?"

That night, as Linda prayed, Rachel didn't just ask God to make her feel better. She renounced the agreement she had unknowingly made with hopelessness and fatigue. She confessed her disappointment with God and how she'd been secretly angry that He hadn't prevented her season of struggle. She gave Him the burden she'd been silently carrying for three years.

Something broke off Rachel. She didn't fall to the floor. She didn't scream or convulse. But the fog lifted. The next morning, Rachel woke up feeling awake for the first time in a long time. The Word burned in her heart again. Worship became adoration, not just singing. Prayer became conversation, not just talking to the ceiling.

This wasn't emotional hype. It was freedom. And it all started with someone discerning what was in the soil.

FRUIT INSPECTORS & ROOT DISCERNERS

Imagine an apple farmer surprised to find apples growing on his apple tree. He picks the fruit, throws it out, and says, "I'm done with apples." Then he comes back the next season and is shocked to find apples growing again.

Believers are like this with root sins. We renounce the fruit and prune the branches. But the roots grow deeper. Unwanted fruit returns in abundance. Until we learn to discern and deal with the root system, the cycle never ends.

Jesus didn't die only to prune your fruit. He died to uproot your old nature, cleanse the soil, and plant His Spirit in you. This is why Paul's words in Galatians 5 draw such a stark contrast:

> The **acts of the flesh** are obvious: sexual immorality, impurity and
> debauchery; idolatry and witchcraft; hatred, discord, jealousy, fits

of rage, selfish ambition, dissensions, factions and envy; drunkenness, orgies, and the like. I warn you, as I did before, that those who live like this will not inherit the kingdom of God. But **the fruit of the Spirit** is love, joy, peace, forbearance, kindness, goodness, faithfulness, gentleness and self-control. Against such things there is no law. Those who belong to Christ Jesus have crucified the flesh with its passions and desires. (vv. 19–24, bold added)

Your life will always bear fruit. *What kind of spirit is feeding the root?*

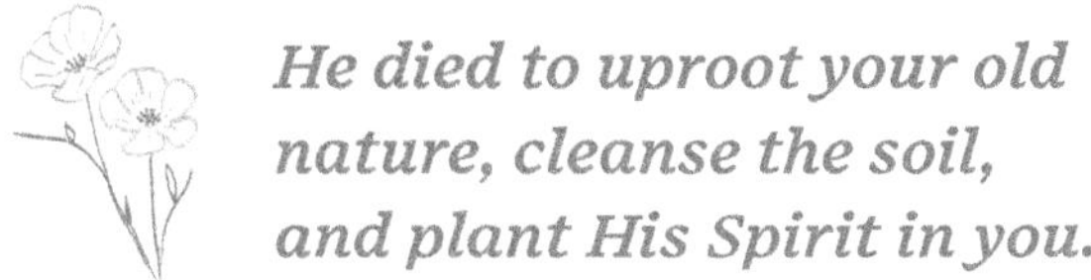

He died to uproot your old nature, cleanse the soil, and plant His Spirit in you.

The Shift in the Battle

Ethan had tried everything, from filters on his phone to accountability groups, weekly confessions, and even fasting. He read every book on purity he could find. He hated who he was becoming, yet he kept going back to the filth like a dog to its vomit. Ethan loved God. He just couldn't get free.

One night, after a particularly crushing relapse, Ethan connected with a leader who listened, prayed, and gently asked, "What if this isn't just a habit you're trying to break? What if there's a spirit fueling this, one that's partnered with parts of you trying to survive pain you never processed?"

That night, something shifted. Ethan didn't just confess. He repented. He renounced the spirits of lust, bondage, deception, and rejection. And more than that, he invited the Holy Spirit to show him what was beneath the surface.

As they prayed, Ethan didn't hear condemnation. He heard invitation. He saw a moment from his childhood that had been buried in silence, an open wound that had never been named. That memory was painful, yes, but it was also the place a lie had taken root. This lie had said, "You're only valuable when you're wanted."

That moment opened the doorway to healing. Through the months that followed, Ethan began to learn how the most immature parts of his heart, the protectors of his image and the soothers of his hurting emotions, were trying to manage pain the wrong way. He learned to stop shaming himself. He invited Jesus to step into all the parts of his heart, and as he did, the strongholds began to weaken.

Ethan stopped focusing on behavior management and started practicing spiritual discernment of any demonic messengers whispering into his soul. He learned to ask, *What am I trying to protect right now? What voice am I listening to? Is this conviction or accusation? Is this discomfort or deliverance trying to break through?*

That's the work of real discernment: casting something out *and* replacing the contaminated roots and patterns as you submit to Christ growing you up.

What's in Your Soil?

If you want to grow in the gift of discerning spirits, start by asking the Spirit to train your spiritual senses. Ask:

- *What am I feeling that doesn't match the moment?*

- *What patterns are repeating in my life, my home, or my church?*

- *Is there a spiritual atmosphere I've grown used to but never questioned?*

- *What do I tolerate in secret that I oppose in public?*

Then allow the Word of God to reveal what's hiding in your soil:

- Is this the flesh? (*sarx*)

- Is this the natural man trying to lead spiritual things? (*psuchikos*)

- Is this from the Spirit? (*pneumatikos*)

- Or is this another spirit entirely?

Here are some indicators to help you discern:

The **flesh** is self-focused, reactive, and driven by immediate gratification. Remember, it produces "obvious" works, including "sexual immorality, impurity and debauchery; idolatry and witchcraft; hatred, discord, jealousy, fits of rage, selfish ambition, dissensions, factions and envy; drunkenness, orgies, and the like" (Galatians 5:19–21).

The **natural man** (psuchikos) operates from human wisdom, emotional reasoning, and natural understanding. It's not necessarily evil, but it can't perceive spiritual things. It tries to manage spiritual problems with natural solutions. This is what happened with the pastor who threw out spiritual-sounding statements from his mind and emotions.

The **Spirit** produces fruit that reflects God's character: "love, joy, peace, forbearance, kindness, goodness, faithfulness, gentleness and self-control" (Galatians 5:22–23). It builds up, brings peace, and always aligns with Scripture. It is birthed in relationship with the Spirit and ministered with the fruits of the Spirit.

Test words with the presence of the fruits and character of the Spirit. Other spirits often masquerade as good but bring confusion, fear, pride, control, or division. They may produce supernatural manifestations, but the fruit is rotten.

THE RESTORED FIELD

Two years after that hunting trip to High Well Ranch, I got a text. This time, Andrew's voice in the text was full of hope: "Just arrived."

I couldn't believe my eyes. The same property that had been a graveyard of death was now teeming with life. Healthy deer grazed peacefully on the same exact ground where we'd once counted carcasses. The soil that had been contaminated with dormant anthrax was now producing abundant grass and life was everywhere.

Here's what I learned. Soil wants to be healthy. When you give it the right conditions and the contamination is removed, it naturally returns to life. The capacity for abundance was always there; it just needed healing."

Today, I keep thinking those words, "Soil wants to be healthy." The same is true for your heart.

The Path to Restoration

The contamination in your spiritual soil, whether buried pain, protective strategies, or hidden shame, is not your true identity. Those wounds have been trying to protect you, as parts of your heart learned to hide or fight or control in order to survive.

But here's the hope: Those parts don't need to be destroyed or cast out. They need to be seen, understood, and submitted to Christ so He can give life.

The wounded child in you who learned distorted or conditional forms of love doesn't need to be silenced. That child needs to be assured that God's enduring, perfect love is here right now.

The fun-seeking or explorative kid in you who learned to make you feel good and have fun through ways that now sabotage your peace and confidence doesn't need to be erased. That is not a literal child in you, is a root of thinking that you developed when you were a kid. When you need comfort, that part of you kicks in gear with efforts to protect you. You need to bring the root of those ways to Jesus. Jesus has so many more meaningful and fulfilling ways to enjoy pleasure and fun.

The gatekeeper-like modes of your nature that were developed very early in life have worked hard to help you survive and keep you protected in life, work, relationships, and all you do. You're not going to benefit at all by beating up the broken ways of your heart. You don't need to be shamed. You need to be valued and matured to know that the Spirit of God is in you, and your help comes from the Lord.

When Jesus said, "Come unto me, all you who are weary and burdened, and I will give you rest" (Matthew 11:28), He wasn't just talking about external burdens. He was inviting every part of your heart, especially the parts that have been working overtime to keep you safe, to find rest in His love.

This is the deep, healing work of discernment: learning to distinguish between the voice of your wounded parts and the voice of your true self, the part of you that is one with Christ. As you grow in this discernment, something beautiful happens. The parts of your heart that have been hiding in the soil begin to trust that it's safe to emerge. The buried and secret part who carries your deepest pain starts to believe they can be seen *and* loved. The protector who has been working so hard to keep you safe begins to understand that Jesus is a better defender than they could ever be.

When this healing happens as the soil of your heart is restored to health, spiritual gifts manifest through the fullness of who you are: integrated, whole, and free. Contamination was never the end of your soil's story. It was merely the compost that would ultimately produce the most beautiful bloom.

Your soil wants to be healthy.

God wants to heal it.

The capacity for abundant life has been there all along, waiting for the right conditions to spring forth. Yes, the superbloom is about what grows from your life, but it's also about the healing of the soil that makes all growth possible.

Your soil wants to be healthy.
God wants to heal it.

CHAPTER 5 STUDY GUIDE

The person without the Spirit does not accept the things that come from the Spirit of God but considers them foolishness, and cannot understand them because they are discerned only through the Spirit. The spiritual person with the Spirit makes judgments about all things.

—1 Corinthians 2:14–15

REVIEW

A toxic superbloom happens when hidden wounds, unprocessed pain, and root sins hidden in the soil of our hearts become activated by the right conditions, even during seasons of blessing, promotion, or favor. The Corinthian church had genuine spiritual gifts that were operating powerfully, yet Paul said their gatherings made things worse. Their soil was contaminated with pride, immorality, division, and chaos.

Paul contrasts two types of people: the *psuchikos* (natural, flesh-governed person) and the *pneumatikos* (Spirit-governed, discerning person). Spiritual maturity is about becoming the kind of person whose life is governed by the Spirit rather than the flesh. True discernment goes beyond identifying visible fruit to exposing invisible roots and the spiritual forces behind them.

Behavior management alone is not enough to find freedom. We must invite the Holy Spirit to reveal what's beneath the surface. The wounded, protective parts of our hearts don't need to be destroyed; they need to be seen, understood, and loved back to health in Christ. When the soil of your heart is restored, spiritual gifts manifest through the fullness of who you are: integrated, whole, and free. Your soil wants to be healthy, and God wants to heal it.

KEY SCRIPTURES

When you come together it is not for the better but for the worse. (1 Corinthians 11:17 ESV)

The acts of the flesh are obvious: sexual immorality, impurity and debauchery; idolatry and witchcraft; hatred, discord, jealousy, fits of rage, selfish ambition, dissensions, factions and envy; drunkenness, orgies, and the like. I warn you, as I did before, that those who live like this will not inherit the kingdom of God. But the fruit of the Spirit is love, joy, peace, forbearance, kindness, goodness, faithfulness, gentleness and self-control. Against such things there is no law. Those who belong to Christ Jesus have crucified the flesh with its passions and desires. (Galatians 5:19–24)

Solid food is for the mature, who by constant use have trained themselves to distinguish good from evil. (Hebrews 5:14)

Come to me, all you who are weary and burdened, and I will give you rest. (Matthew 11:28)

GROUP DISCUSSION

1. What are some obvious signs a person's life is being influenced by toxins beneath the surface? What should be the visible fruit when someone is living with healthy spiritual soil?

2. Paul said the Corinthians' church gatherings were "for the worse" despite having real spiritual gifts. How can believers discern whether spiritual activity is producing genuine transformation or just impressive displays?

3. What's the difference between sin that's actively being committed and root issues that lie dormant until activated? How does understanding this difference change the way we pursue spiritual health?

4. What does it look like practically to operate from the Spirit (*pneumatikos*) rather than human wisdom or emotional reasoning (*psuchikos*)?

5. How can we as a group help each other grow in spiritual discernment without becoming suspicious or critical? What's the difference between healthy spiritual awareness and unhealthy spiritual paranoia?

PERSONAL REFLECTION

1. If your spiritual life were a ranch, what would be the current condition of your soil? Are there areas where you've noticed patterns of toxicity or contaminated growth?

2. What things might be lying dormant in your heart that could potentially "superbloom" under certain conditions? What would it look like to address these proactively rather than reactively?

3. Think of a recent situation where you felt spiritual confusion or unrest. What might the Spirit have been trying to show you about what was going on beneath the surface?

4. Instead of simply managing symptoms, what would it look like to allow the Holy Spirit to reveal and heal the root system of the recurring issues in your life?

PRAYER

Father God, we invite You to search the soil of our hearts. Reveal what lies dormant beneath the surface and expose any wounds, pain, or sins that need to be addressed. Help us recognize contamination without fear or shame. Train our spiritual senses to discern between flesh, natural wisdom, other spirits, and Your voice. Uproot anything that isn't of You. We surrender the wounded parts of our hearts and ask You to heal us so we can walk in the fruit of Your Spirit. May we learn to trust Your love and rest in Your presence as whole and free people of God. In Jesus' name, Amen.

6

TONGUES

The Bunny Slopes of Spirit-Led Prayer

Prayer is not bending God to my will, but it is bringing my will into conformity with God's will, so that His will may work in and through me.

—E. Stanley Jones

Anyone who speaks in a tongue edifies themselves.

—1 Corinthians 14:4

Why would we be afraid of a gift that God says builds us up?

—Francis Chan

HAVE YOU EVER been snow skiing? If you've looked at a trail map at any resort, you've seen this key:

- Bunny slopes: Beginner practice area

- Green circle: Easy

- Blue square: Intermediate (more difficult)

- Black diamond: Advanced (most difficult)

- Double or triple black diamond: Extremely difficult, potentially dangerous (essentially, "You'll die if you try").

I've only been skiing once, back when I was a 6'4", 315-pound college football player. A group of us went to Snowshoe Mountain in West

Virginia. And yes, there were females on the trip. What happens when guys are around females? We show off.

Every. Single. Time.

Put six guys in a gym, and we'll play basketball for hours just fine. Bring one female in, and someone's going to sprain an ankle trying to impress her.

There I was, having never skied in my life but thinking, *I can roller skate. I bench 400 pounds. I squat 600. How hard can skiing be?* So instead of starting slow, I strapped on my boots and went straight to the blue slopes with the crew.

Big mistake.

Blue isn't beginner.

Blue means you better know what you're doing. And I didn't. At all. Most importantly, I didn't know how to stop. Instead of asking someone, I just assumed I'd figure it out on the way down.

Picture the scene. Families are enjoying a quiet, peaceful, snow-covered day on the mountain when a 315-pound snow monster suddenly comes barreling toward them, screaming, "MOVE! MOOOOOVE!"

It was terrifying for *everyone.*

I couldn't stop.

I had no clue how to turn or slow down either.

The only thing I could do was warn people loudly, crash into a snowbank, and spray ice like a freight train. After two days of a destroyed ego, two bruised hips, a jacked-up back, and far too many terrorized children, I hated skiing. I was done. I decided to stay inside the lodge and drink coffee for the rest of the trip.

But then one of the guys in the group suggested something different: "Why don't you go to the bunny slopes?"

"The what?"

"The bunny slopes."

I found the bunny slopes. It's right by the kids' pre-ski school.

If there were texts with emojis back then, the palm-to-face emoji would need selection here.

I walked over there, and sure enough, the spot was filled with eager five-year-olds and cautious great-grandparents. I almost went back to my coffee, but I decided to humble myself and learn how to point my skis inward, balance, slow down, and perform traditional slope etiquette like a normal human.

After just two hours on the bunny slopes, I was having fun. And after lunch, I was back on the blue square. Only this time, nobody's grandma was in danger.

WHICH DO YOU RELATE TO?

In Chapter 1, I briefly referred to differing beliefs regarding the gift of tongues. Most people relate to one of the following four views:

- **Cessationist**—You believe that tongues ceased in the first century and that the gift was a supernatural ability to speak real foreign languages without study for the sole purpose of evangelism.

- **Personally Cessationist**—You are open to others having the gift, but you have no interest operating in the gift yourself. You believe that if you have the gift, then you'll just start operating in it without choice, teaching, or guidance like they did in Acts 2.

- **Open But Cautious**—You believe the gifts likely still exist, and you think the gift of tongues includes a personal affinity for languages, Bible translations, and other natural things. However, you're cautious. When you desire the gift, you mostly wait for something to happen to you. Perhaps you've tried it, and you're even eager for it at times. You may not understand what it is or why it matters, but you've grown to tolerate it in others as long as there is an interpreter present.

- **Charismatic and Exclusive**—You pray in tongues often, but you think it's only for those who've been baptized in the Spirit. You may even lean toward tongues being proof of having the Holy Spirit dwell in you.

- **Mature in the Gift**—The gift of tongues is a regular part of your Spirit-led prayer life and personal devotion. You do not think it is a sign of salvation or even spiritual maturity, but you do believe it is available for every believer by faith.

Where are you on that list? Do you have another category that I didn't think of? I want to invite you to the bunny slopes of Spirit-led prayer. It's not a gift for the elite. Actually, none of the gifts are for the elite. All the gifts are for those who need God's power to do what they cannot do on their own.

A FOURFOLD FRAMEWORK

Most people think being Spirit-filled just means having access to the gifts and dynamic power of the Spirit that comes with the gifts. But if you don't understand how the Spirit distributes, directs, and manifests those gifts, you'll either misuse them or reject them entirely. That's why Paul starts his teaching on spiritual gifts in 1 Corinthians 12 with a framework most people skip:

> There are diversities of gifts, but the same Spirit. There are differences of ministries, but the same Lord. And there are diversities of activities, but it is the same God who works all in all. But the manifestation of the Spirit is given to each one for the profit of *all*. (vv. 4–7 NKJV)

This explains so much of the confusion and division around the gifts today. Paul doesn't begin with prophecy, tongues, or healing. He begins with how the Spirit works. This four-part breakdown is foundational to how we understand the gifts of the Spirit. Paul is not being redundant; he's being surgical.

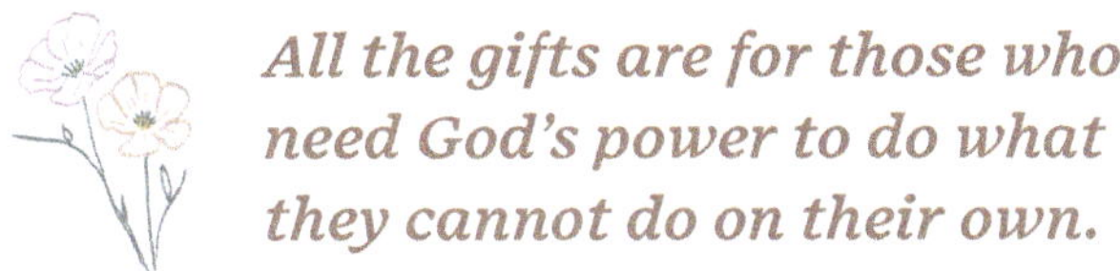

All the gifts are for those who need God's power to do what they cannot do on their own.

The Fourfold Framework of the Spirit
(1 Corinthians 12:4–7)

Greek Phrase/English Phrase	What It Means
diaireseis charismatōn "diversities of gifts"	Varied Spirit-given abilities
diakoniōn "differences of ministries"	Unique contexts or roles for service
energēmatōn "diversities of activities"	Varied impact levels or outcomes
phanerōsis tou pneumatos "manifestation of the Spirit"	Visible expression of the Spirit's presence

Greek Phrase/English Phrase	Why It Matters
diaireseis charismatōn "diversities of gifts"	You don't have just one tool in the shed.
diakoniōn "differences of ministries"	The same gift looks different on different platforms.
energēmatōn "diversities of activities"	Some gifts will flow in quiet prayers, others in firepower.
phanerōsis tou pneumatos "manifestation of the Spirit"	Every gift reveals the living Spirit, not just a human ability.

Let's make this practical:

- There are **multiple gifts**, or grace-powered abilities, available to each believer.

- There are **different ministries**, or platforms and service roles where those gifts show up. Some ministries are public, and some are private. Some occur in packed stadiums, some occur in a conversation with a friend and some occur under a tree in a bush village. Ministries can include serving, counseling, helping, and administrating.

- There are **different activities**, or varying levels of working, power, and fruit. Some activities bear significant visible impact, such as life-altering miracles, while others are so subtle that you're not sure if it's even the Spirit.

- All these are **manifestations** of the Spirit himself being made visible through you. He makes His presence known in the ministry.

This matters because most people either

- limit the gifts to dramatic moments (see the next section), or

- don't recognize the Spirit's activity unless it's loud, public, or platformed.

Some people reject the gift of tongues not because it isn't biblical but because they've collapsed all four categories into one narrow expectation. If it doesn't look like Pentecost with fire and languages and thousands of conversions, they assume it's fake.

But here's the truth: Some manifestations of the Spirit happen on stages. Others happen in living rooms, cars, hospital rooms, or even in your bedroom alone, with tears and groanings too deep for words.

Remember what we learned about the soil in Chapter 5? The same Spirit who helps us discern what's growing in our hearts also distributes His gifts through different soils, different ministries, and different levels of activity. And in Chapter 7, we'll explore the surge of faith that activates these gifts across all four dimensions, not just in one dramatic way.

A word of knowledge might manifest as a quiet impression during coffee with a friend (gift + ministry + activity + manifestation). The same gift might manifest as a bold declaration in front of hundreds (different ministry, different activity, same gift, same Spirit). Both are authentic manifestations. They're just different expressions of the same divine reality.

If we don't understand this framework, we'll either discredit the supernatural or idolize it. When we do understand it, it becomes a lens for discernment, as well as a check on our spiritual pride, fear, and skepticism. When I first started praying in the Spirit, I compared it to Pentecost. But this framework helped me realize I was expecting black-diamond ministry and activity when God was giving me bunny slopes gifts that were just as real and just as powerful.

This framework changes everything about how we approach spiritual gifts.

- Instead of asking "Do I have the gift?" you ask, "Holy Spirit, how do you want to make yourself known through me?"

- Instead of waiting for the right ministry platform, you recognize that every conversation is a potential ministry context.

- Instead of expecting the same level of activity every time, you stay sensitive to how the Spirit wants to work in each moment.

Tongues truly is the bunny slopes gift because it teaches us to recognize and trust the Spirit's manifestation in its simplest form. Once you learn to discern the Spirit's presence in private prayer, you can recognize His work in every area of life. When your soil is healthy and surrendered, this is how the Spirit flows.

The Problem with a Black-Diamond Definition

One morning, as I was praying and preparing to teach on this gift to a diverse group of believers, I asked God, "Why is this gift so controversial?" I sensed Him reply, *Because their definition of tongues is black diamond.* I lit up and began to dig in even more because this statement was pivotal for me as a pastor. I love helping people discover the riches of things that seem too complicated.

The gift of tongues is different from the others. Many people think it's a rare, elite, and miraculous ability to speak in foreign languages for evangelism. So, when they hear someone pray in the Spirit privately, they dismiss it. When they overhear it publicly, they get defensive and start pointing to the Bible asking, "Where's the interpreter?" They may even mock it as "bunny slopes gibberish."

I humbly believe many are measuring the wrong thing. The real black diamond in the kingdom isn't public gifting. It's private surrender. Every gift is cultivated on the bunny slopes of surrender and humility.

Tongues doesn't start on the black-diamond slopes of evangelistic declarations of praise. It's not exclusive for those who can utter praises to God in a known foreign language. If it were, then who could verify the interpretation? If tongues is an ability to speak in an unstudied foreign language, then someone interpreting it would not be exercising a gift. They would simply be bilingual and thus able to interpret and translate.

The gift of tongues is a spiritual language that sounds like utterances known only to God. If anyone steps out and prays in the Spirit, this gift always begins by faith on the bunny slopes of humble, Spirit-led prayer. It starts by becoming like a child and yielding your mouth to God in faith.

WHAT ARE TONGUES, REALLY?

Let's clear the fog and establish a working definition. Tongues is the Spirit praying or praising through you in a spiritual language or utterance that you don't understand but that reaches God perfectly. It strengthens your spirit, affects your future, activates spiritual warfare, deepens worship, aligns you with God's will, and helps you intercede when you don't know what to pray.

Tongues isn't gibberish. It's surrender. It's Spirit-empowered communication beyond your understanding. Let's look at what Scripture says:

> For anyone who speaks in a tongue does not speak to people but to God.… they utter mysteries by the Spirit. (1 Corinthians 14:2)

> Anyone who speaks in a tongue edifies themselves.
> (1 Corinthians 14:4)

> I would like every one of you to speak in tongues.
> (1 Corinthians 14:5)

> If I pray in a tongue, my spirit prays. (1 Corinthians 14:14)

> I thank God that I speak in tongues more than all of you.
> (1 Corinthians 14:18)

These aren't one-off ideas. This is Paul's normal language.

A Warning to the Inner Critic

If we are entirely honest, some of us hear the word *tongues* and cringe. I get it. I grew up cessationist too. But today, I know many believers from different backgrounds who pray in tongues.

Be careful not to dismiss a gift from God just because it doesn't fit your definition. The crowd at Pentecost mocked the disciples and said they were drunk. But Peter corrected them very quickly: "These people are not drunk, as you suppose. It's only nine in the morning! No, this is what was spoken by the prophet Joel" (Acts 2:15).

Some of you might say, "Well, Joel never mentioned tongues." You're right. But Acts 2 connects the dots, showing how tongues is actually a form of prophecy:

> All of them were filled with the Holy Spirit and began to speak in tongues as the Spirit enabled them. (v. 4)

> This is what was spoken by the prophet Joel:

> "In the last days, God says,
> I will pour out my Spirit on all people.
> Your sons and daughters will prophesy,
>   your young men will see visions,
>   your old men will dream dreams.
> Even on my servants, both men and women,
>   I will pour out my Spirit in those days,
>   and they will prophesy." (v. 16–18)

Notice that Joel never mentions the gift of tongues. He mentions prophecy. Tongues is very prophetic because it's the Spirit of God speaking praises to God through your mouth. Tongues is the Spirit of God speaking to God through you.

That's amazing. It's not weird. It's worship. You need it. Otherwise, God wouldn't make it available by faith.

WHAT REALLY HAPPENED IN CORINTH?

Understanding cultural context changes everything. Corinth wasn't just any city. It was home to one of the most spiritually elite cultures in the Roman Empire. Right next door was Delphi, which housed the famous Temple of Apollo with its elite female prophet, the Pythia.

These women would go into trances and speak mysterious utterances under the influence of the Greek god, Apollo, giving oracles that people traveled from across the empire to hear. It was all about spiritual status and mystical elitism. If you could access the Pythia, you were somebody.

This spiritual elitism had infected the Corinthian church. It's like when a church today gets so focused on having "powerful" services that the gifts become performance pieces rather than genuine ministry. I've seen churches where prophetic preaching becomes a show. It's highly entertaining with coached and programmed clapping by the crowd. The staff sits in the front section to fill the room with pre-planned responses to manipulate the room. I've seen worship become so choreographed that the production team and arts leaders are bullied by senior pastors to get the lights, audio and smoke just right in order to evoke the right manipulated response to sing, or cry, or even come to the altar. Each of these are used to manufacture the presence of God. And we've all seen people compete to have the most "anointed" prayer in prayer circles.

This may appear to be a new thing; however, if you examine Corinth closely, you'll see this was happening with them first. Real activity and real gifts were corrupted by spiritual pride. Apparently, only certain elite women were allowed to prophesy in their gatherings. They held branches as signs they were receiving divine revelation. They'd give spiritual interpretations through tongues and other manifestations, but it was all for show and status. My personal belief is this spiritual elitism corrupted their gatherings. (There's substantial historical evidence for this.)

Here's where it gets interesting: The church in Corinth wasn't flawed because they operated in dynamic spiritual gifts. They were flawed because they were trying to mix spiritual gifts, ministry, and worship with pagan mysticism and spiritual elitism. But Paul doesn't tell them to put a stop to the gifts. He never once hints toward a black-diamond definition, that tongues is an unstudied language miraculously spoken for the purpose of evangelizing foreign tribes.

The elite dominance of spiritual mysticism was overtaking their meetings, which Paul declares to "do more harm than good" (1 Corinthians 11:17). These gatherings were chaotic, prideful, and performance-based. That's not the Spirit. That's show.

But Paul never tells them to stop praying in tongues. He doesn't even tell them their praying in tongues isn't real. He tells them that it is immature because it happens in front of others without an interpretation, which means it has no love in it. It is "only a resounding gong or a clanging cymbal" (1 Corinthians 13:1).

In fact, he later writes, "I thank God I speak in tongues more than all of you" (1 Corinthians 14:18). He is trying to teach the Corinthians how to use the gift properly with love, humility, and order.

PRAYING IN THE SPIRIT: PURE SPIRITUAL WARFARE

Ephesians 6 lays out the full armor of God. Most people stop at the helmet of salvation and the sword of the Spirit, but Paul doesn't:

"And pray in the Spirit on all occasions with all kinds of prayers and requests" (Ephesians 6:18). Praying in the Spirit is a powerful way to activate the armor. It's a foundation for how we do battle.

I believe that praying in the Spirit is the most dynamic weapon in spiritual warfare. Why? Because you don't know what you're saying. It's not about your knowledge or eloquence. There's zero glory in it for you. It's about surrendering your tongue to the Holy Spirit, allowing Him to pray God's will through you.

In Romans 8:26–27, Paul writes, "The Spirit helps us in our weakness.… the Spirit himself intercedes for us through wordless groans." When you don't know what to pray, the Spirit does. And He prays through you.

I used to argue, "It says He intercedes *for* us, not through us." I no longer make that argument, though, because it ignores every other verse in Scripture about praying in the Spirit and the Spirit praying through us. It's at least wise to consider that the Spirit delights in partnering with your humility and praying through you and for you at the same time. This is not a stretch like I used to make it out to be.

When you pray in the Spirit, you don't know what you're saying, and you don't know when the Spirit is interceding through you. God loves working things through His people, though, and it's incredible to imagine all the things that happen for good that are unknowingly connected to you praying in the Spirit. You can't brag about interceding for someone and God answering your prayer when it's the Spirit interceding through you in tongues.

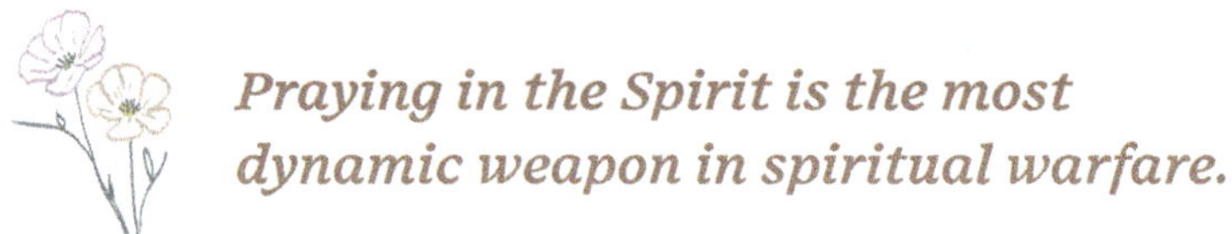

Praying in the Spirit is the most dynamic weapon in spiritual warfare.

A Story from Kenya

Before I share this story, it's important to note that I'm not saying this was directly related to any one person's intercession or praying in the Spirit. But it does make me wonder how many times God intervenes through wordless groans when we don't know how to pray for a situation.

Through our partnership with Mission Maasai, we have dozens of family churches in the bush villages of southern Kenya. One week, a team of our pastors went to a village but were run out by a witch doctor who was intimidating to some and verbally abusive to all of them.

The next week, Timothy, our lead pastor, said the Lord was leading the team to return to that same village. They showed up prepared to preach the gospel while also expecting warfare again. But this time, everything was different.

The village leaders approached the pastors and greeted them warmly. When the pastors asked about the man who had run them out the previous week, the village leaders replied, "He was trampled by an elephant this week." The witch doctor's family came to Pastor Timothy and said, "We want your God." That day, twenty-eight people got saved, including the family that once resisted them.

Our board and church family are always interceding in prayer for that region. Some of that intercession happens in English. None of us knows if intercession is also happening by people who pray in tongues, though I believe it is. I believe some of the most dynamic things on earth happen through wordless groans when we don't know what to pray.

Could it be that while our pastors were facing opposition, the Spirit was interceding on their behalf through believers thousands of miles away in ways we'll never fully understand? I believe so. You never know who you're interceding for when you pray in the Spirit.

Why Some Never Step Onto the Slopes

If we're not praying at all, we're most likely not going to wake up fluent in tongues. As a pastor, I've met many people who attend church but don't pray at all, not even in English. I've even heard of one of my close friends who began to pray in tongues before he ever prayed in English. (He's been a pastor for almost fifty years now.) We're all at different stages of experience and understanding.

As you worship, study, pray, and seek God, know this: Your prayer life as a whole matters. Tongues is designed to be a part of your prayer life. It's designed by God to build you up. It may seem like the top of the mountain, but it's actually an invitation to start climbing. It's the bunny slopes for surrender.

DAILY PRACTICE: MY PRAYER FLOW

Most mornings, I go to the gym around four. That's where my prayer starts. After that, I usually arrive at my office and put on instrumental music with no lyrics. I always start off my devotion time with the Word open, and I begin praying in the Spirit and singing to the Lord. This whole time is mostly listening. I always make notes of everything the Spirit brings up, but I avoid studying, reading, researching, or anything else that distracts me.

Sometimes the Spirit will bring up a dream I had the night before. Sometimes He brings up a burden for my family or someone in the church. Sometimes He addresses something that needs correcting in me. (That happens most of the time.)

Then I move on to the Bible, and I'll spend an hour or so of praying in English, singing, praying in the Spirit, writing, and memorizing Scripture. Sometimes I lie down. Sometimes I fall asleep.

Yep. I admit it. The good news is this time isn't a formula. It's just a rhythm. And praying in the Spirit is layered throughout my whole day. It lets my entire being know, *I am a spirit, I have a soul, and I live in a body. I live my life directly connected with a real God in an unseen realm.*

When I pray in the Spirit, my anxiety immediately disappears. It's impossible to pray in the Spirit and be worried or anxious at the same time. Praying in the Spirit literally shuts off the anxious parts of your thinking, and singing in the Spirit does the same thing with musical notes. That's even more powerful in changing your state of being and ushering you into God's presence in the Spirit.

THE QUESTION THAT CHANGES EVERYTHING

One day, I listened to Dr. John Piper share about his personal experience in desiring the gift of tongues. He said, "I do not believe I've authentically spoken in tongues." He also said, "I used to sit in the car outside church singing in the Spirit, but I knew I wasn't. I was just making it up. And I said, 'This isn't it.'"[1]

I used to say the exact same things. Dr. Piper's language and approach are endearing to me, and I respect his humility and integrity with the Word. I don't intend any disrespect at all. I just need help understanding something. I would love to ask Dr. Piper, "How would you know

---

1 John Piper, "What Is Speaking in Tongues?" *Desiring God,* January 17, 2013, https://www.desiringgod.org/articles/are-prophecy-and-tongues-alive-today.

if you had authentically spoken in tongues? How would you know if you really had sung in the Spirit?"

This is a powerful question I use with people who enter a conversation saying things like, "I don't think my wife loves me anymore." At some point, I ask, "How would you know if she did?" Or if someone says, "I don't think I'm supposed to stay in my job," I ask, "How would you know if you were supposed to stay?"

Dr. Piper has asked for the gift of tongues. He's tried operating in the gift. But I wonder if he's evaluating it against a certain expectation, maybe even a black-diamond one that is not accurate. If it is accurate, it greatly contradicts my personal experience and everything I've seen in the Word of God.

If I were to have a conversation with Dr. Piper and ask him these questions, I don't know how he'd respond. I do know he'd be humble, though. Most of the people I've spoken to who align with his interpretation will shift the conversation to the doctrine that supports the notion that tongues is something "you know is real when you do it."

I've been there, but I'm not there anymore. Friends, you don't have to be "taken over" by the Spirit, and you don't have to wait for something elite to happen that is miraculous for other people.

Tongues is not for others. It's for you. The Spirit doesn't possess you and take over your mouth. He partners with you and prays through you. Paul writes, "The spirits of prophets are subject to the control of prophets" (1 Corinthians 14:32). It's not, "I couldn't help it." It's, "I chose to surrender, and I prayed in the Spirit by faith."

GETTING STARTED: PRACTICAL FIRST STEPS

So how do you actually start? It's simpler than you think, but it requires the same humility I needed on those bunny slopes. It's also not a formula or pattern. It could start for you right now with zero prep. You can just start. But if you want a guide you can trust, here it is. (Just don't turn it into a formula!)

- **Get with God.** Tongues isn't a public gift initially. Start where you sense God leading you to be. It's not about feeling safe or private; it's about surrender.

- **Begin worshipping.** Start with familiar praise and worship. Let your ears hear your mouth connect with God. Seek Him and enter His presence.

- **Open your mouth and speak.** Yes, it really is that simple. Just open your mouth and speak by faith. Praise God with your spirit. Don't analyze it. Don't judge it. It's for God, and it builds you in ways nothing else can.

- **Don't evaluate. Just continue.** For some, it's so refreshing they never want to stop. For others, it might feel awkward at first, like those initial moments on the bunny slopes when nothing feels natural. But keep going. Trust God, trust His Word, and trust His purposes.

- **Make it a regular practice.** This is a gift for you. Like skiing, it becomes more natural and powerful the more you do it. The goal isn't to sound impressive or mystical. The goal is surrender. You're giving God permission to pray through you in ways your mind can't orchestrate.

Don't Wait for Black Diamond

All gifts start with bunny slopes surrender. Surrender your mouth. Surrender your need to understand everything. Surrender your pride.

When you trust God with your tongue, you're not becoming weird. You're becoming available. Tongues isn't childish, though it certainly is childlike. Instead of being spiritual enough or mature enough, this gift is about being surrendered enough. When the Spirit sees surrender, He always speaks. If you are a follower of Jesus Christ, you're already qualified. But are you willing to trust God with your mouth, your pride, and your need to understand everything before you step out?

Tongues is the bunny slopes gift because it's where you learn to trust God with the most powerful thing you possess: your words. Once you learn to trust Him in that place of private surrender and intimate prayer, you discover that what seems like the smallest gift actually becomes the foundation for everything else He wants to do through you.

And once you learn to trust God with your tongue in private prayer, you will learn that the same Spirit who prays through you also wants to speak through you to encourage others. That's where the gift of prophecy comes in, as the Spirit's encouragement flowing through surrendered hearts. Again, it's not about elite revelation. It's about surrender. The superbloom you've been waiting for might just be on the other side of surrendering your tongue to the Spirit of the living God.

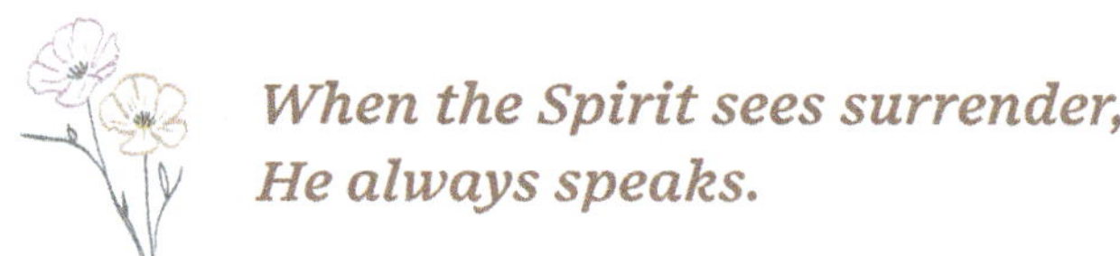

When the Spirit sees surrender,
He always speaks.

CHAPTER 6 STUDY GUIDE

For anyone who speaks in a tongue does not speak to people but to God. Indeed, no one understands them; they utter mysteries by the Spirit … I would like every one of you to speak in tongues.

—1 Corinthians 14:2, 5

REVIEW

Tongues is the bunny slopes of Spirit-led prayer, a humble starting place for learning to partner with the Holy Spirit. Like skiing, the goal isn't to perform on black-diamond terrain but to learn balance, trust, and surrender. Paul begins his teaching on spiritual gifts with the fourfold framework: diversities of gifts, differences of ministries, varieties of activities, and the same Spirit manifesting through all (1 Corinthians 12:4–7). Gifts are God-given abilities, ministries are the contexts where they're used, activities are the levels of power and fruit that vary by moment, and manifestation is the Spirit himself revealed through us.

When we collapse these categories, we confuse expression with maturity, assuming dramatic equals divine. Paul corrected the Corinthians not by canceling the gifts but by restoring love, order, and discernment. Tongues is not about spiritual status; it's about surrender. In private prayer, it trains us to sense the Spirit's presence in every area of life.

Praying in the Spirit strengthens intercession and warfare when we don't know what to pray (Ephesians 6:18; Romans 8:26–27). It teaches us that true maturity begins in humility, as we trust God with our words, our hearts, and the unseen work He's doing within us.

KEY SCRIPTURES

There are diversities of gifts, but the same Spirit. There are differences of ministries, but the same Lord. And there are diversities of activities, but it is the same God who works all in all. But the manifestation of the Spirit is given to each one for the profit of all. (1 Corinthians 12:4–7 NKJV)

For anyone who speaks in a tongue does not speak to people but to God. Indeed, no one understands them; they utter mysteries by the Spirit. (1 Corinthians 14:2)

The Spirit helps us in our weakness … the Spirit himself intercedes for us through wordless groans. (Romans 8:26–27)

All of them were filled with the Holy Spirit and began to speak in other tongues as the Spirit enabled them … "This is what was spoken by the prophet Joel." (Acts 2:4, 16)

GROUP DISCUSSION

1. Where have you seen confusion arise because people expected "black diamond" expressions of a gift rather than "bunny slopes" beginnings? How can the fourfold framework bring clarity?

2. What modern versions of spiritual elitism do you see in church culture? How can we preserve a culture of love and service rather than performance?

3. Read 1 Corinthians 14:2–5, 14. What purposes of tongues do you observe for the individual and for the gathered church? How do love and order guide public use?

4. In what ways can praying in the Spirit cultivate humility, courage, and discernment in everyday life?

5. How do Ephesians 6:18 and Romans 8:26–27 shape your view of intercession when words fail? What practices help you "pray in the Spirit on all occasions"?

PERSONAL REFLECTION

1. Where is God inviting you to leave performance and step onto the bunny slopes of simple, surrendered prayer?

2. Which part of the fourfold framework do you tend to overlook: gifts, ministries, activities, or manifestation? How has that shaped your expectations?

3. When you consider 1 Corinthians 14:32, what would it look like for you to cooperate with the Spirit rather than wait for something to "overtake" you?

4. Identify one setting this week (commute, walk, lunch break) where you will set aside time to pray in the Spirit and listen. What might obedience look like if the Spirit prompts you afterward?

PRAYER

Father, thank You for giving us good gifts through Your Spirit. Teach us to begin with humility as we release pride, comparison, and fear. Train our hearts to welcome every authentic manifestation of Your presence. Fill our gatherings with love and order and let our private surrender bear public fruit that builds others up. As we pray in the Spirit, strengthen our inner life, align us with Your will, and intercede through us when we lack words. We yield our minds, our mouths, and our motives to You. Make us faithful stewards of every gift so that Jesus is honored in all we do. In His name, Amen.

7

SURGE OF FAITH

The Turbo Gift for Breakthrough

Faith … is the art of holding on to things your reason has once accepted, in spite of your changing moods.

—**C. S. Lewis,** *Mere Christianity*

With faith I can do all things; without faith I shall neither have the inclination nor the power to do anything in the service of God.

—**Charles Spurgeon,** *Morning and Evening*

THERE'S A FLY on the window.

He's not scared. He's not lost. He sees the light and feels the air. He wants the freedom just on the other side of the glass. So he buzzes. He slams. He tries again. Harder. Louder. Faster. No matter how many times he hits the window, he can't break through.

What the fly doesn't realize is that two feet to the right, there's a wide-open door. But he's so locked into what he thinks is the way out, he never senses it. Exhausted, he'll die on the windowsill, not because there wasn't a way out but because he couldn't see it.

I was like the fly trying to help Cindy.

THE STORY THAT CHANGED EVERYTHING

In the fall of 2003, I met a woman who would change the way I understood the Spirit of God and the battle for freedom. Her name was Cindy, and she was a director of a large advocacy company in our city. She was also a significant leader in the Satanic cult in North Texas. You'd never know it if you met her.

I had only been the pastor of the Shannon Oaks Church for a few weeks and had just finished preaching a message exposing the rising influence of witchcraft and Wicca and how darkness was flooding homes through the internet and media. It was bold, but I felt the Spirit's conviction resting on the room. Many responded to the altar call.

As the congregation of about 500 was singing, one of the altar team members came over and said, "Pastor Jeff, that woman on the end wants to talk to you." Cindy had made her way to the front row. Body shaking. Knees locked together. Feet tapping. Hands clenched. Eyes lasered on the floor.

I walked over, unsure of what I was walking into. She wouldn't look at me at first. Her whole body was tight, trembling. I gently knelt beside her, placed my hand on hers, and said, "I'm Jeff. What's your name?"

"Cindy," she said so quickly that her lips only opened for half a second.

"Cindy, what do you need?"

She finally looked me in the eyes. Jaw locked. Lips still tightened.

"Part of me wants to kill you. And part of me wants to be free." She quickly looked around the crowd and then put her head back down. She started shaking even more.

I had no clue what to do. I was thirty years old with zero experience in deliverance ministry. I didn't know very much about spiritual gifts. I didn't know how to deal with demonic influences. All I had were personal victories, a genuine heart for people, and Scripture.

So I said the first thing I could muster with conviction: "Cindy, look at me now." She looked up and relaxed enough to listen. I strongly said, "I want to meet with you in my office at 2:00 today. I'm not afraid of what's in you. 2:00, okay?" That was it. I didn't want to pray for Cindy right then because I didn't know what to pray. I had no faith for ministry in that moment. I didn't even know how close things were to a full-blown demonic manifestation.

Over the next few months, I walked with Cindy through some of the darkest things I've ever seen. She had been in the Satanic cult her whole life, and her roots were scary deep in it. I cannot even begin to describe it all.

I immediately brought other women into this ministry situation with me. We did everything we knew to do. We counseled Cindy's family. We dealt with altars, multiple personalities, and borderline personalities. We drove to literal graveyards hours away to deal with traumatic memories. We talked through severe abuse, torment, dissociation, self-harm, suicidal voices, perversions, and a host of toxic relationships and attractions. We saw demons manifest many times. It was exhausting.

We were loving Cindy well, but nothing was breaking through. We gave her time, grace, and the love of Jesus. My default is seeing the parts of a person that many can't see and ministering grace there with unconditional acceptance and redeeming love. I was doing everything I had learned through years of good therapy and ministry.

It all worked for me, and it helped Cindy some. But it wasn't enough.

In fact, it started to backfire. The longer I tried to love her out of darkness without power, the more emotionally attached she became. The more I tried to lead her toward healing, the more codependent the whole dynamic became. The whole process was draining my spirit, like a fly slamming into a window over and over with the open door just a few feet away.

The Moment Everything Shifted

It had been months of fighting for Cindy's freedom. I was worn out, depleted, asking God what to do. Two of us were talking with Cindy in the office that day when, suddenly, something surged in my spirit. At that point, I hadn't had any experiences that people would call a "baptism in the Spirit," and I had never knowingly operated in the gifts of the Spirit. But at that moment, I knew He was there. The Spirit of God was present to act. It wasn't emotion. It wasn't effort. It was a surge of faith. (This experience would later serve as evidence to me that the gifts are the Spirit's and that He can administer them through anyone He wants.)

Cindy was so deep in demonic bondage that she was convinced God was evil and Satan was a victim. She concluded that God is the one who created evil and didn't give Satan grace. One of her alternate personalities, the dominant one who had a name, gave a long, emotional rant, and then the Spirit of God moved in mighty power.

The shift wasn't in my technique or her circumstances; it was the Spirit of God making Himself known through the gift of faith in my spirit. Instead of trying to love Cindy out of darkness through human wisdom, I suddenly knew that God was present to act. Instead of emotion or desperation, I had a supernatural certainty that the Spirit wanted to move in that moment. So, I stopped counseling and started declaring. I stopped analyzing and started prophesying.

I knelt in front of Cindy to remove any form of dominant position, just like at our first meeting at the altar months earlier. But this time, I wasn't uncertain. No psychology. No diagnosing. I was ministering in the Spirit.

"I'm done with this," I said, not to Cindy but to the atmosphere, and I began to prophesy. The Holy Spirit spoke the sovereign love of God over her. He declared the redeeming love of God for her. He preached the gospel with power to her. It was Him through me.

Everything shifted. A calm came over Cindy that I had never seen in her. Tormenting fear stopped manifesting immediately. I spoke life over her. I declared who she really was. I called out her identity, her purpose, her design. I told her what God had already been forming in her.

Something broke. It was powerful. She supernaturally saw God as redeeming love. She saw a perfect God who created a world with the potential to fall and a redemptive plan that included His own sacrifice and mercy. She saw Satan as the deceiver (and verbally said so).

I led Cindy in a prayer of repentance and surrender. No fanfare. No drama. Just clarity, power, boldness, and faith. Within days, Cindy was baptized in front of the whole church. We were all nervous about that because she was told she would die in the water if she ever did it. Well, she did die in the most powerful way. She died to the demonic allegiance to the enemy and her own flesh. And truthfully, when I took her under the water, the power in the building flickered. The electricity literally went out for a few seconds. It lit the whole room up in more ways than one.

And the next day? Dead animals showed up on the front lawn of the church.

I'm serious. This happened.

Cindy's story isn't tidy. There were still spiritual attacks, marriage challenges, old associations popping up, and many intense moments over the years that followed. Several women in our church "adopted" Cindy. They stayed with her through so much growth. A small group of believers literally made Cindy's whole family their mission to love.

When the Spirit of God moves, it's not a counseling session; it's a surge of heaven. In my office that day, I experienced the Spirit in the gift of faith and heard Him speak through me. I've never ministered the same since. It's not trying harder. It's pure relational and submitted faith.

This is the gift of faith, the turbo gift.

It's a surge that ignites everything else, including discerning of spirits, prophecy, words of knowledge and wisdom, boldness, authority, healings, and miracles. Like tongues, it's about surrendering to the power that's already moving through the open door.

The gift of faith operates through the same fourfold framework we learned about in the previous chapter:

- There are diversities of gifts. Faith manifests differently in different people.

- There are differences of ministries. Some operate in faith in healing rooms, others in boardrooms, and still others in everyday conversations.

- There are diversities of activities. Some faith surges lead to dramatic breakthroughs, while others build to quiet confidence.

- They are all the manifestation of the same Spirit.

This is crucial because many people miss the gift of faith the same way they miss tongues: waiting for black-diamond ministry and activity when God is offering pure and simple manifestations that are just as real and just as powerful.

When the Spirit of God moves, it's not a counseling session; it's a surge of heaven.

WHAT IS THE GIFT OF FAITH?

In the past several years, this gift has been present almost every day. Every morning I pray, I sense faith surge in me. I always pray and worship until I sense the presence of the Lord and faith rise up. He usually activates some other form of ministry, message, or prompting for me to do by faith. I know it's Him because I know Him. I know His voice, and I'm sensitive to His Word and what he brings to my mind and heart in prayer.

When I've heard others describe their experience of this gift, they say things like, "Faith began to rise up in my spirit, and I suddenly felt strong in the Lord. It was like the mighty power of God was present unlike normal times." They'll also describe a surge in confidence in the presence of God, and they'll carry a strong assurance in their whole being that the Lord is present to work His will and His love in a situation.

The gift of faith is not the same as saving faith.

It's not general belief. It's also not optimism, positive thinking, or even deep confidence in God's promises. It is a manifestation of the

Holy Spirit himself through a supernatural surge of faith. It is a Spirit-empowered infusion of bold assurance that activates, accelerates, and amplifies everything else the Spirit is doing in and through you.

You know the Spirit is present and about to move. It's not a dopamine high. It's not an adrenaline rush. It's not just an energy. It is the Person of the Holy Spirit moving. It's spiritual, relational, sober-minded, and full of His presence and power.

Another Black-Diamond Misconception

Once again, people think the gift of faith is a black-diamond experience or some rare, elite ability to perform dramatic miracles in front of crowds. When they feel a surge of spiritual boldness or divine conviction, they dismiss it as natural enthusiasm or emotional hype. But that's like waiting for a lightning storm instead of recognizing the power that flows through the electrical outlets in your house every day. The gift of faith isn't always dramatic. More often, it's the quiet surge that gives you supernatural confidence to pray for someone, speak a word of encouragement, or step into a situation where God wants to move.

Many people miss this gift because they're looking for Mount Carmel when God is offering them everyday moments of supernatural empowerment. They want fire to fall from heaven, but they won't recognize the gentle breeze that carries divine authority.

Don't wait for black-diamond faith to fall on you. Start recognizing the surges of faith that are already available on the bunny slopes of everyday ministry.

Biblical Foundation

Interestingly, the Bible doesn't give us a clear textbook definition of the "gift of faith."

Paul lists it in 1 Corinthians 12 as one of the gifts distributed by the Spirit, but he never explains it. Instead, Scripture gives us a host of examples where someone is suddenly filled with boldness, clarity, power, or prophetic conviction. That's when everything shifts.

The gift of faith is not about results. It doesn't guarantee any desired outcome. The only guarantee is in your spirit as you sense, *The Lord is here and present to move.*

Think about Stephen, who, filled with the Spirit, stood before the Sanhedrin and saw heaven open. That didn't convert the crowd; it led to his martyrdom. But the gift of faith fueled the sermon and his boldness.

Think about Peter. One day he denied Jesus three times, and then a few weeks later, he stood up at Pentecost and preached with fire. That wasn't textbook preaching you learn in seminary. That was a word of knowledge and prophecy that led to 3,000 salvations in one day.

This surge of faith, this moment of unmistakable spiritual power, often shows up right before breakthrough, deliverance, or a miracle. The Old Testament gives us a picture of this in Isaiah 11:2. It describes the Spirit of the Lord resting on the coming Messiah, including "the Spirit of counsel and might." That phrase isn't about physical strength. It's not just courage. It's dynamic, God-breathed power to act on heaven's impulse.

The gift of faith is like plugging a regular extension cord into a lightning bolt. Sure, it will light you up, but more importantly, it charges you for the ministry the Lord has for you in the moment or season. It is the Lord's presence being made known in power in real time. And when it moves through you, things shift in you. You will know it because you will experience the presence of the open door, and you'll move from trying harder to trying faith.

Recognizing the Real Thing

How do you know when it's the gift of faith versus natural boldness, enthusiasm, or adrenaline? Here are some markers:

- The gift of faith brings supernatural peace, not nervous energy. When faith surges, you're not anxious about the outcome; instead, you're confident in God's presence.

- It produces clarity, not confusion. You know what to do, what to say, or how to pray with unusual certainty.

- It focuses on God's glory, not your performance. You're not trying to look spiritual or impress people; you're simply responding to what the Spirit is doing.

- It always aligns with Scripture and the character of Christ. True faith never contradicts God's revealed nature or written Word.

- It feels less like effort and more like partnership. Instead of trying to stir yourself up, you're caught in the current of something heaven is releasing.

The gift of faith doesn't operate in a vacuum. Notice how the same Spirit who gives faith manifests through different people in different contexts and activities, but the markers remain consistent.

Recognizing the Gift of Faith in Action

What You Feel	What It Activates	Ministry Context	Typical Activity
Sudden Certainty	Prophecy, Word of Knowledge	Private or Public	Speaking God's Heart
Surge of Boldness	Healing, Deliverance	Ministry Situations	Praying or Speaking with Authority
Holy Conviction	Discernment, Wisdom	Counseling, Leadership	Addressing Root Issues
Holy Urgency	Intercession, Spiritual Warfare	Prayer Contexts	Sustained Prayer
Peaceful Confidence	All Gifts Subtly	Everyday Conversations	Natural Ministry

Do you see the gifts more clearly now? This will unfold in the coming chapters as well. The gift of faith isn't a one-size-fits-all experience. It's the same Spirit working through the same framework of different gifts, different ministries, different activities, and different manifestations of God's presence and power.

This is why some people experience faith as a quiet surge of confidence during a conversation, while others feel it as supernatural boldness in a public setting. It's about recognizing when the Spirit is present to act and partnering with Him in that moment.

The key is learning to discern the difference between human effort and divine empowerment across all these contexts. When you understand this framework, you stop waiting for black-diamond experiences and start recognizing the bunny slopes surges that are available every day.

Faith and the Soil of Ministry

In Romans 12:6, Paul gives us a clue about saving faith and the gift of faith: "We have different gifts, according to the grace given to each of us. If your gift is prophesying, then prophesy in accordance with your faith." Some translations say "in proportion to your faith" (CEB,

ISV). Notice that Paul assumes everyone who is saved has faith, but he also acknowledges that some have more faith in the soil of their lives. There's a baseline faith that all believers possess, and then there's something else, something extraordinary.

Connecting Back to Chapter 5

We have already explored what's lying beneath the surface of your heart: the spiritual toxins, the exiled parts, the unhealed places where deception hides, the sincere faith, the gift of the Spirit, salvation, new life, and the dormant power of resurrection. We saw how *pneumatikos* living means more than having gifts; it means being spiritually mature and discerning. It is in tune with the Spirit, not just the stage.

The danger is that you can operate in spiritual gifts without faith, ministering from the toxic elements in the soil instead of from the Spirit of God. When I was young and early in ministry, I was often tempted to minister in the flesh because I usually felt like I had nothing to give but compassion, Scripture, and some well wishes. Those things help people, but they lack power.

Even as I grew in human wisdom, I was able to use my flesh to look at a person, discern their birth order by their apparent emotional needs, and give something most would discern as "spot on." But to the Lord, it would be unspiritual.

Thankfully, it terrifies me to speak something "of the Lord" when it's merely psychology. When I sense something like this, I always pray, *Holy Spirit, are You here? What are You doing?* Every time, within seconds, I'll sense a surge of faith, and it will be evidenced with honesty and purity.

The surge of faith brings spiritual maturity to every gift. Yes, you can prophesy in the flesh, but it'll be rooted in psychology, not the Spirit. You can also lay hands for healing and say spiritual things without faith, but it'll be about your power, appearing spiritual, or wanting admiration.

That's what was happening in Corinth. They had all the gifts, but Paul says they were not *pneumatikos*. They were immature, fleshly, and spiritually tone-deaf. That's why the gift of faith matters so much. It's the difference-maker, the power-shifter. It takes ministry from the natural (*psuchikos*) to the supernatural (*pneumatikos*).

The gift of faith is like flipping the switch from striving in your flesh to surrendering in the Spirit. When faith surges, it reveals the open door and activates the other gifts with life-giving power, always through the fourfold framework. The same prophetic word might manifest through different ministries (private conversation vs. public declaration) and different activities (gentle encouragement vs. bold correction), but it's always the same Spirit making Himself known.

TURBOCHARGING THE OTHER GIFTS

I call faith the turbo gift because instead of standing alone, it partners. When the Holy Spirit manifests His presence through the gift of faith, He always activates something more than a feeling. It might be prayer, worship, giving, serving, preaching, prophecy, healing, or miracles. The Spirit manifests through faith and supercharges all other ministry needed in the moment. He awakens, accelerates, and amplifies the gifts.

When the Spirit begins to surge within you, He will not allow His gifts to stay dormant. They come alive, though they do not all function the same way. Some bring clarity. Some bring change. Some do both. I've come to see the gifts of the Spirit, especially those empowered by the gift of faith, fall into two primary movements:

- **Insight gifts** bring revelation. They give you heaven's perspective in real time.

- **Impact gifts** bring transformation. They bring heaven's intervention into the moment.

Insight reveals. Impact restores. One sees. The other shifts. And when faith flows through them, both explode with purpose.

These categories aren't rigid. They simply help us understand that the Spirit doesn't just want to work through us; He wants to grow in us. Every believer can grow in sensitivity, surrender, and strength in these gifts. Some may walk in greater fruit or more frequent expressions of one or more, but the invitation is the same for all: Eagerly desire the gifts and follow the surge of faith when it comes.

The Five Insight Gifts

These are the gifts that allow you to see, know, and speak by the Spirit.

- **Prophecy**—Faith turns vague impressions into bold declarations. When the Spirit makes Himself known, His presence stops your wondering if you should say something and activates you to sense the word to start declaring. It's almost always what God has already made clear in your spirit. Faith gives it weight, timing, and clarity.

- **Word of Knowledge**—Faith gives you courage to speak what you know only by the power of God. It replaces any fear of being wrong and locks you into the moment to serve and help others experience being seen and known by the Lord.

- **Word of Wisdom**—Faith clarifies and releases the power of the fear of the Lord. Greater than strategy, it's a revelation from God of how to move forward in the fear of God. You're not just offering advice; you're delivering blueprints. Faith helps you recognize divine timing and the right next step for someone's breakthrough.

- **Discerning of Spirits**—Faith keeps you from fear or pride when you see something spiritually. You're not intimidated by what's demonic, and you're not puffed up when something holy is revealed. Faith helps you stand steady, speak clearly, and respond with authority and humility regardless of what you sense.

- **Interpretation of Tongues**—Faith turns indiscernible language into clear prophetic ministry. You don't translate a language you know by intellect; you interpret what the Spirit is saying through an utterance by the Spirit. Faith helps you trust that the impression you're receiving is from the Lord and that it carries real weight for the moment.

The Two Impact Gifts

These are the gifts that release healing, power, and tangible disruption of the natural order.

- **Gifts of Healings**—Faith surges when the Spirit nudges, *Pray now*. It's not emotion or desperation; it's divine conviction.

You sense healing is available in that moment. You don't have empty, rehearsed words. You sense a surge of faith to minister healing regardless of the outcome. You won't worry about failing or appearances, and it won't be legalistic or insensitive. It will be the Lord, and you'll know it.

- **Working of Miracles**—Faith breaks natural limits and creates holy disruption. Instead of managing the impossible problem, you're confronting it. Faith gives you the courage to step out of logic and into the supernatural. It's heaven's authority confronting earthly impossibility. You will have zero fear of failure when you sense the gift of faith manifesting.

THREE THINGS THE GIFT OF FAITH EMPOWERS

The gift of faith doesn't replace or overpower the other gifts. It activates and empowers them. Here are three things the gift of faith empowers:

1. Spirit-Empowered Conversations

Amos 3:7 says, "Surely the Sovereign Lord does nothing without revealing his plan to his servants the prophets." The Spirit of God loves shifting ordinary conversations into dynamic breakthroughs. This has happened hundreds of times in my life.

I have to come back to a foundational prophetic word and a surge of faith that changed my world. I mentioned in the introduction that shortly before COVID-19 changed the world, Larry Stockstill stood on our new church property with two of our elders and me and gave a prophetic word regarding the next five years and the superbloom that would come.

We were just having a conversation about how the Lord provided our new land and the massive mountain ahead of us. We couldn't see how He was going to provide or how we would even walk out the next steps. And we had no clue that it was going to be even harder than we imagined.

Within six weeks, we lost our meeting location. We didn't worship on Sunday mornings together for the next twenty-three months. We almost sold the land, but God provided in supernatural ways, just as He had spoken through Larry. We received over $12 million for our new building in the middle of a global crisis and economic collapse.

During that five-year period, I remembered that prophetic word and repeated it at least 100 times. I told it to my own heart, and I brought it up in board meetings. We were walking on the Word of God and clinging to the prophetic encouragement He sent us.

Anchor Church is a miracle of God. We broke ground a few months later, and by the end of the fifth year, Anchor grew from 142 adults to over 5,000 people. How? That superbloom was birthed in a prophetic conversation that the Lord activated through Larry.

My friend sensed a surge of faith. He stopped the talk and shifted to ministry in the Holy Spirit, declaring by faith what he sensed the Lord speaking. That ministry revealed God's mighty hand working in us. It also changed how we move forward as stewards of God's grace.

Even now, toward the end of 2025, we're entering a $71 million multi-phased expansion of our facilities, ministries, university, and global church-planting initiatives. All of it is birthed and cultivated in prophetic conversations.

We no longer operate by strategic plans. We don't hire outside consultants to help us figure things out. This is not arrogance; this is refusing to operate as a strategy-first church.

Before the pandemic, I was always loaded with a strategic plan or the ability to get one fast. I made a lot of money coaching organizations and businesses in developing and activating strategic plans. But now, thanks to God's supernatural grace saving us, I am driven by His hand to lean into discerning the activity of the Lord humbly. When we sense faith is present and we're united in His leading, we're learning to operate by faith, not by the wisdom and plans of men.

My friends, you are one ordinary conversation away from someone else's breakthrough. When the Spirit speaks, it becomes a Spirit-empowered conversation.

2. Spirit-Empowered Change

More of the same usually leads to more of the same. If you always do what you've always done, you're always going to get what you've always gotten. So, if you want to experience a superbloom in your life, God's going to move you by His Spirit to do what you've never done before. He's going to use the gift of faith to move you out of your comfort zone and into a God-zone where He starts to minister through you.

Look at what happened when Ananias received his breakthrough conversation. In Acts 9, we see this ordinary man receive a supernatural surge of faith that led to extraordinary change.

In Damascus there was a disciple named Ananias. The Lord called to him in a vision, "Ananias!"

"Yes, Lord," he answered. (v. 10)

Notice faith in the soil of Ananias' life. He wasn't an apostle, a prophet, or a writer of Scripture. Ananias was just an ordinary Jewish believer living in Damascus, yet he was so familiar with the voice of the Lord that he immediately recognized it.

The Lord told him, "Go to the house of Judas on Straight Street and ask for a man from Tarsus named Saul, for he is praying. In a vision he has seen a man named Ananias come and place his hands on him to restore his sight." (vv. 11–12)

That's a word of knowledge because Ananias couldn't have known this specific information on his own.

Ananias tested the spirit:

Lord … I have heard many reports about this man and all the harm he has done to your holy people in Jerusalem. And he has come here with authority from the chief priests to arrest all who call on your name. (vv. 13–14)

That was actually a smart move. You should never receive a word, even from your own heart, without testing it.

Then came the surge of faith: "But the Lord said to Ananias, 'Go!'" I believe the moment Ananias heard that directive, the Spirit of might moved on him. He went from fear to faith, from hesitation to holy boldness.

Then Ananias went to the house and entered it. Placing his hands on Saul, he said, "Brother Saul, the Lord—Jesus, who appeared to you on the road as you were coming here—has sent me so that you may see again and be filled with the Holy Spirit."

Immediately, something like scales fell from Saul's eyes, and he could see again. (vv. 17–18)

Paul received physical healing, but notice what else happened: "He got up and was baptized, and after taking some food, he regained his strength." (vv. 18–19). That's emotional and spiritual healing. That's why Scripture calls them "gifts of healings" (plural). There are different kinds of healing that flow when the gift of faith activates.

Here's what I love about this story: The gifts of the Spirit enable believers to do much more with much more power and much less effort. One ordinary man, prompted by God and activated by supernatural faith, became the catalyst for the conversion of the greatest missionary in church history.

This gift of faith doesn't just impact prophetic conversations and ignite healing and miraculous change. It is designed to bless the entire community of faith.

3. Spirit-Empowered Community

Phil Robertson, the founder of Duck Commander and the patriarch of the Duck Dynasty world, passed on May 25, 2025. He was seventy-nine years old. I was with the family at his memorial service in West Monroe, Louisiana, and it was incredible to see all social media posts from people all over the world who were impacted by his faith.

Several posts included a picture of three people I've known my whole life. On the left is Phil Robertson, with long hair, a long beard, sunglasses, and a white t-shirt. In the middle is Phil's sister Jan, and on the right is my childhood preacher, Bill Smith.

When Phil was 26–28 years old, he was no longer the elite Louisiana Tech football star quarterback. He was a married man with three young boys. He was also an adulterer, a drunkard, a drug addict, and an abusive, domineering, and violent husband. He owned a small bar in southwest Arkansas, and he described his former self as "a rough, good-for-nothing scoundrel."

One day, the Holy Spirit prompted Jan to talk to her preacher, Bill Smith. She told him, "If you go talk to my brother and convert him to Christ, he will reach thousands."

Bill asked, "Who's your brother?"

"Phil Robertson. He owns a bar in southwest Arkansas."

Moved by the Holy Spirit, just like Ananias, Bill went to that bar. The first time, Phil intimidated him, shut him down, and ran him off. Bill went by faith and left by wisdom.

Over time, things got worse for Phil and his family. One day, Phil broke, and in desperation, he connected again with Bill. The pastor shared the gospel with Phil, who surrendered his whole life to Christ. It was a powerful conversion that led to a total restoration of his family.

Nobody knew that this ordinary drunkard in southwest Arkansas would become someone who impacted millions and millions of people. His son Willie has shared this story many times, saying, "My aunt told that preacher, 'If you convert Phil, he'll convert thousands.' How did she know that? Because she was led by the Spirit."

Willie continued: "I'm thankful to those two people who lived changed lives. They didn't just live a life that got changed years ago and then try to go to church and do the best they can. They actively pursued Phil and Kay. When they came to the Lord, their kids grew up in the church. I'm one of them. If that doesn't happen, I don't meet Korie. We don't have these kids. All these ministries don't happen. There's no Duck Commander. There's no Duck Dynasty. None of that happens. The evil one wins. But for two people living changed lives, led by the Spirit, who got in a car, drove to that bar, and preached the gospel—hundreds of millions of people have been exposed to the gospel."

That's what happens when ordinary people respond to the surge of faith. Spirit-empowered community starts to manifest. The Spirit changes our worlds.

THE SPIRIT OF MIGHT IS MOVING

We've seen breakthrough conversations that activate prophetic dreams and strategic vision. We've seen breakthrough change through healings and miracles. And we've seen breakthrough community where ordinary believers impact millions.

I believe that right now in our church family and in many all over the world, God is preparing to activate worshippers, artists, musicians, writers, pastors, kingdom business leaders, servant leaders, and church multipliers. Each person's heart is going to catch fire. It's not just about one preacher gathering people through sermons; it's about the whole Church being activated to move throughout our areas of influence.

The superbloom is happening, not just in numerical growth but in spiritual activation. Not just more people in seats but more people on fire with the purposes of God. The gifts of the Spirit enable believers to do much more with much more power and much less effort. We don't have to strive harder. The Spirit of might is coming upon ordinary people and doing extraordinary things through them.

Your Surge Is Coming

Maybe you've been waiting for breakthrough for years. Maybe you've been sowing and serving and believing, but you haven't seen the harvest yet. Maybe you've been feeling like that fly pressed against the window, trying harder but not getting through.

Your surge of faith is coming. Expect it. Cultivate your heart for His presence. The same Spirit of might that came upon Samson, David, Gideon, Jesus, and Stephen wants to come upon you. The same Spirit that moved on Ananias to heal the blind and transform the violent wants to move through you.

This gift has not ceased. If it was needed to start the Church, it is absolutely needed 2,000 years later in a world where there are more distractions and evil than ever before in human history.

Ask the Spirit of God to make this great gift known to you. The same Spirit that prompted Jan Robertson to speak to her preacher, who went to that bar and changed the trajectory of millions of lives, wants to use your ordinary conversations for extraordinary purposes.

You are one conversation away from someone else's turning point. You are one surge of faith away from breakthrough change. You are one Spirit-led moment away from your own revival fire.

The question isn't whether you're qualified. Ananias wasn't an apostle. Jan Robertson wasn't a preacher. Bill Smith was just a local pastor. Phil Robertson was a drunkard who became a voice for the gospel to millions.

The question is, *Are you willing to recognize the gift when the Spirit of God is moving?* Are you willing to go when God says go? Are you willing to speak when the Spirit prompts? Are you willing to step out of your comfort zone and into the God-zone?

The measure of faith is the soil you've been cultivating through prayer, Scripture, and surrender. The gift of faith is the downpour that's coming to activate everything God has planted in you.

Your superbloom is about becoming a catalyst for breakthrough in others. It's about moving from consumer to contributor, from receiver to reproducer, from maintainer to multiplier. The surge of faith is the turbo gift that activates everything else. And I believe it's coming to this generation, to this Church, and to you.

Once you learn to recognize and respond to the surge of faith, you will discover something amazing. The same Spirit who gives you supernatural boldness also wants to give you supernatural insight. The gift of faith activates the impact gifts, and it also empowers the insight gifts that help you see what God is doing and speak what God is saying. That's where prophecy comes in, not as mystical fortune-telling but as faith-empowered communication of God's heart to His people.

Are you ready for the downpour?

You are one surge of faith away from breakthrough change.

CHAPTER 7 STUDY GUIDE

Now to each one the manifestation of the Spirit is given for the common good.... to another faith by the same Spirit.

—1 Corinthians 12:7, 9

REVIEW

The gift of faith is a supernatural surge of bold assurance that moves us from striving in our own strength to operating in God's power. It is not saving faith, optimism, or adrenaline. Instead, it's a manifestation of the Holy Spirit that produces a clear, peaceful certainty that God is present to act. This surge shifts ministry from the natural to the supernatural.

Like tongues, this "turbo gift" functions within the fourfold framework of different gifts, different ministries, different activities, and different manifestations of the same Spirit. Faith may surface quietly in everyday moments or powerfully in public ministry. It fuels both the insight gifts (prophecy, words of knowledge and wisdom, discerning of spirits, and interpretation of tongues) and the impact gifts (healings and working of miracles). Wherever the Spirit moves through faith, revelation and transformation follow.

The gift of faith is not reserved for rare, dramatic moments. It is available to every believer who yields to the Spirit. It always brings peace and clarity, aligns with Scripture, and glorifies God rather than self. When believers cultivate healthy spiritual soil through prayer, surrender, and obedience, they begin to recognize daily bunny slopes surges that lead to Spirit-empowered conversations, change, and community.

KEY SCRIPTURES

The Spirit of the LORD will rest on him—
    the Spirit of wisdom and of understanding,
    the Spirit of counsel and of might,
    the Spirit of the knowledge and fear of the LORD.
(Isaiah 11:2)

We have different gifts, according to the grace given to each of us. If your gift is prophesying, then prophesy in accordance with your faith. (Romans 12:6)

In Damascus there was a disciple named Ananias. The Lord called to him in a vision, "Ananias!"

"Yes, Lord," he answered.

The Lord told him, "Go to the house of Judas on Straight Street and ask for a man from Tarsus named Saul, for he is praying. In a vision he has seen a man named Ananias come and place his hands on him to restore his sight."

"Lord," Ananias answered, "I have heard many reports about this man and all the harm he has done to your holy people in Jerusalem. And he has come here with authority from the chief priests to arrest all who call on your name."

But the Lord said to Ananias, "Go! This man is my chosen instrument to proclaim my name to the Gentiles and their kings and to the people of Israel. I will show him how much he must suffer for my name."

Then Ananias went to the house and entered it. Placing his hands on Saul, he said, "Brother Saul, the Lord—Jesus, who appeared to you on the road as you were coming here—has sent me so that you may see again and be filled with the Holy Spirit." Immediately, something like scales fell from Saul's eyes, and he could see again. He got up and was baptized, and after taking some food, he regained his strength. (Acts 9:10–19)

GROUP DISCUSSION

1. How can we recognize the difference between human effort and a Spirit-given surge of faith? What are some of the markers of the gift of faith?

2. Using the fourfold framework, how can we help each other identify and affirm the diverse ways the Spirit moves among us?

3. In what ways does the gift of faith bring unity rather than competition among believers? How can we create space for both quiet and bold expressions of faith?

4. How might the body of Christ and the world benefit if we learned to celebrate bunny slopes surges of faith just as much as dramatic breakthroughs?

5. How can we cultivate the kind of spiritual soil that recognizes and responds to the gift of faith? What barriers (fear, pride, unbelief) might prevent us from responding?

PERSONAL REFLECTION

1. In what areas of your life are you like the fly hitting the window through effort? What fears or habits tend to keep you from acting when you sense a surge of faith?

2. Romans 12:6 talks about prophesying "in proportion to your faith." How would you assess the measure of faith in the soil of your life? What practices help cultivate that soil?

3. Which of the three areas (Spirit-empowered conversations, change, or community) do you most need to experience? What would it look like to remain alert for the Spirit's leading in that area?

4. Who in your life might need encouragement that could come through your obedience to a simple prompting of faith this week?

PRAYER

Father God, thank You for the gift of faith that activates and empowers Your work in and through us. Teach us to exchange our striving in the flesh for surrender to Your infinite wisdom and power. Help us to embrace both the quiet and bold manifestations of Your Spirit. Activate the insight and impact gifts through our lives for the good of others and the advancement of Your kingdom. Fill us with courage to step through every open door You provide, to speak when You give us the words, and to move when You say go. In Jesus' name, Amen.

8

WHEN GOD SPEAKS

The Misses, The Mystery, The Moments

I believe in Christianity as I believe that the Sun has risen: not only because I see it, but because by it I see everything else.

—**C. S. Lewis,** *Is Theology Poetry?*

Try the man who says he is inspired. … Whatever power comes from the Spirit of Divinity belongs to the Lord.

—**Shepherd of Hermas**

Do not quench the Spirit. Do not treat prophecies with contempt but test them all; hold on to what is good, reject every kind of evil.

—**I Thessalonians 5:19–22**

IN 2024, MOTHER'S DAY was on May 12th. How do I know? That morning, I preached a sermon on the woman at the well, a story in John 4 about divine insight and the prophetic moment Jesus shares with a stranger. During the message, I told a story about a powerful moment I had at Haywire Restaurant in Plano, Texas.

Sky was our waitress. She wore jeans, a tucked-in shirt, and cowgirl boots. She had an off-white, slouch-style outback cowgirl hat and the swag of one who owns the room. But the moment Sky walked away from our table after taking our drink order, I had a vision and impression that turned out to be from the Lord. I took out my phone and wrote down this exact phrase:

She's young, but she's a matriarch in her family. She's not from here. She moved here to get some relief. Tell her the Lord brought her here and she doesn't need to feel the pressure of holding things together back home. Tell her 1 Peter 5:7: "Cast all your anxieties on the Lord because He cares for you."

Sky came back a few times to take care of us, and after she took our orders, I sensed the timing was right. I said, "Sky, I'm Jeff. I'm a pastor in McKinney. When I saw you earlier, I had an impression that I felt was from the Lord, and I want to tell you something encouraging."

I gave her the exact word. Sky immediately teared up in the middle of that packed restaurant. Her lip quivered. Then she grinned and nodded: "Pastor, you have no idea. You have no idea." She wiped her eyes and walked away, clearly moved.

Later, it was time for our check. But instead of bringing us that slip of paper, Sky brought out a massive piece of bread pudding with a huge ball of ice cream and loaded drizzle on top. She said, "This is on the house. That word was the Lord. You made my day."

I shared about that prophetic moment with Sky in the first point of my sermon that Mother's Day. Just a few hours later, my world was rocked. My son was involved in an altercation in a public place right after his senior Baccalaureate. People screamed, "Call the police!" and "You're going to jail!"

My son panicked, left the state, and totaled his truck. He was missing for hours. I arrived at the scene of the wreck and saw blood on the cracked windshield. I started an intense search in the woods surrounding his truck. A group of friends from the area joined me, calling out my son's name, begging God to help.

My mind was in all the dark places. Angry. Sick. Devastated. For over four hours, I believed in my heart that my son was dead. Then we found him, unconscious but alive. *Thank God.*

We spent the next nine days in the hospital, and truly, we have seen the hand of God in it all. But my first response after I sobered up from all the adrenaline was this: *God, if You were willing to give me such a clear, specific, powerful word for a waitress at a restaurant that morning, why didn't You give me anything about my own son?*

Have you ever felt that tension? That frustration? That mystery? There's a name for it: theological dissonance.

DEFINING THE TENSION

What do you do when the God you trust, the God you hear, doesn't say the one thing you feel you needed to hear most? What happens when your spiritual experience and your lived reality feel out of sync? If you've ever said, "God, I thought You would have told me," you're not alone.

Theological dissonance is the collision between expectation and experience. It can sound like:

- *Why do I get words for strangers but not warnings for my family?*

- *Why did I feel led to pray for someone else's healing but didn't see my own breakthrough?*

- *Why do I hear encouragement for others but silence when I cry out for direction?*

It's closely related to cognitive dissonance, that uncomfortable tension when belief and reality don't match. Think of the smoker who admits, "I know this is killing me," as they light up. Or the person who says, "I trust God," but secretly avoids prayer because of unhealed disappointment.

If we're honest, dissonance can lead to self-protection: *If I stop expecting to hear God, I can't be disappointed when I don't.* But what starts as protection quickly becomes isolation.

We drift. We disengage. We say we trust God, but we pull back from intimacy with Him. We fear missing it. We fear looking foolish. We fear getting hurt again.

Through wrestling with these questions, I've learned that the very tension that makes us doubt our ability to hear God might actually be preparing us to hear Him better. Understanding when and how God speaks isn't about having all the answers; it's about faithfully partnering with whatever piece He chooses to give you.

WHY DIDN'T GOD TELL ME?

> When she reached the man of God at the mountain, she took hold of his feet. Gehazi came over to push her away, but the man of God said, "Leave her alone! She is in bitter distress, but the LORD has hidden it from me and has not told me why." (2 Kings 4:27)

Even Elisha, the miracle-working prophet of Israel, found himself in a moment of confusion. A grieving woman stood before him, aching with loss, and Elisha had no prophetic word. No insight. *Nothing.* That moment has helped me more than most sermons because it's so real.

Elisha wasn't broken. God wasn't absent. But there are times in this life when insight seems to vanish. The lines go silent. The discernment fades. The God who speaks now doesn't. And it stings.

There is hope, though. You're not alone in that silence. Many of the greatest heroes of faith wrestled through seasons where the voice of God felt missing. So, if you're in one of those seasons, you're not broken or failing. You're being invited deeper.

Let's walk through four common moments where theological dissonance can show up as your heart cries out, *God, why didn't You tell me?* With each one, I want you to see that you're not the first. And you're not stuck.

1. Seeing for Others, Blind to Yourself

You hear God with clarity for others, but when it comes to your own life? Silence. That was me on Mother's Day. Maybe that's you right now. You can pray with insight for a friend's business, but you feel lost in your marriage. You can sense direction for your child, but you feel aimless in your calling. You can get prophetic words in prayer gatherings, but you feel nothing when crisis hits at home.

Elisha knew that feeling. The Shunammite woman stood in front of him in agony, and he had nothing from the Lord. No word. No warning. No wisdom.

If you've ever felt that ache, know this: You're not abandoned. You're not disqualified. Sometimes the Lord invites us to follow Him without clarity so that we lean into trust. He is still with you, even in the blind spots. He's drawing you closer, not pushing you away.

2. Silence in Crisis, Clarity in Calm

There are moments where hearing God feels effortless, like during worship, in the quiet, or while journaling. You've sensed His guidance in transitions and even heard Him for others. But then life falls apart through loss, betrayal, or anxiety. Suddenly, you hear nothing. It can make you question *everything.*

Look at Job. His friends had a lot to say, but God stayed silent for thirty-seven chapters. And when He finally spoke, He didn't give Job a blueprint. He gave Job a revelation of Himself.

Job didn't respond, "God, You are cruel for being silent and not telling me Your plans." No, he said, "I know that you can do all things; no purpose of yours can be thwarted" (Job 42:2).

Never forget that in suffering, despair, or painful uncertainty, nothing matters more than your relational presence with God. No matter what, He is your hope. He may not answer every question, but He never wastes the silence. He uses it to reshape your view of Him. And when He reveals Himself, it's always enough.

3. Selective Accuracy

Have you ever seen powerful prophetic moments with clear words, accurate details, and dreams confirmed? But then some global disaster happens like a pandemic or a gruesome war, and the prophetic world seems caught off guard. You wonder, *If so many people can hear about who I'll marry or what job I should take, how did nobody see this coming?*

The truth is that prophecy has never been exhaustive. In Acts 11:28, a prophet named Agabus "stood up and through the Spirit predicted that a severe famine would spread over the entire Roman world." But not every storm was predicted, and not every tragedy was prevented.

Paul writes, "For we know in part and we prophesy in part" (1 Corinthians 13:9). That's not failure; it's design. God never intended prophecy to be a replacement for His sovereignty or Scripture. I see it like taking supplements for greater faith and devotion to Him. Prophecy is an invitational gift for building up others, not for obtaining the foreknowledge of the supreme God of the universe. It's not about predicting everything. It's about partnering with what He chooses to reveal.

4. Blessings Prophesied, Loss Unspoken

Have you ever been frustrated by all the prophetic words calling out blessing, love, success, favor, promotion, and open doors? If so, it's probably because you never hear any words about the heartbreak that blindsided us, the betrayal that wasn't warned, or the moral collapse no one mentioned.

Walking through that can shake your confidence in prophetic ministry, but look again at Paul. The greatest apostle faced beatings, shipwreck, imprisonment, and, yes, betrayal. He was told he would suffer, but not every moment was explained in advance.

God is not hiding the hard things to punish you. He's growing you into someone who walks by trust, not just by insight. I'm perfectly fine with all the positive words about His promises. We need hope and a joyful vision of His power, love, provision, protection, and favor. It's true, and it's real.

Don't get stuck in the slump of despair and let toxic negativity make you critical of encouraging words. Personally, I don't want to be in a room with people giving out negative words. As soon as they do, I'm immediately going to prophecy living hope, and it will be mighty.

No matter how negative anyone got with the apostle Paul, he roared back things like, "I consider my life nothing" (Acts 20:24) and "to live is Christ and to die is gain" (Philippians 1:21). You couldn't kill his joy with negative words.

Get over this one as soon as you possibly can. Hope is alive and well. The best is always ahead in Christ. Amen.

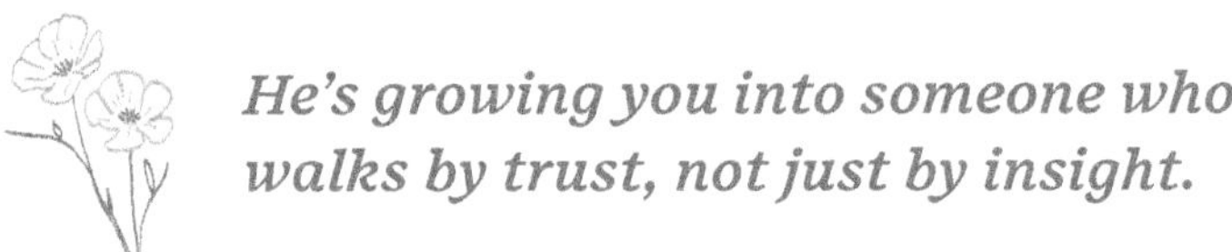

He's growing you into someone who walks by trust, not just by insight.

THERE'S HOPE FOR YOU

When I sat on a massive box in the middle of the woods and believed in my heart that my only son was dead, I spent those terrible moments in the belly of despair. One good thing did come from that experience, though: I now know how I'll respond on my darkest day. I was in it. I had questions. But I have also been to the bottom many times, and I know hope is always alive and well.

I know the Word. I know Psalms. I know Job. I know the Garden of Gethsemane. I know the resurrection tomb. I know the upper room. I know the prison cells. I know the persecution and the loneliness.

But I also know the God above all gods and the King above all kings. I know the One in whom I live and move and have my being. I don't play games with faith.

I know the intense meaning behind Paul's declaration:

> But whatever were gains to me I now consider loss for the sake of Christ. What is more, I consider everything a loss because of

the surpassing worth of knowing Christ Jesus my Lord, for whose sake I have lost all things. I consider them garbage, that I may gain Christ and be found in him, not having a righteousness of my own that comes from the law, but that which is through faith in Christ—the righteousness that comes from God on the basis of faith. I want to know Christ—yes, to know the power of his resurrection and participation in his sufferings, becoming like him in death and so, somehow, attaining to the resurrection from the dead. (Philippians 3:7–11)

These words are deep in my soul. I don't have to look them up to quote them. They're "living and active, sharper than any two-edged sword" (Hebrews 4:12 ESV). They cut through my soul and my spirit, my bones and my marrow. They judge the depths of my heart. My conscience is laid bare before His living Word. And in my darkest moments, they carry me when I have no revelatory word. Instead, I have something much greater: I have the living Word of God inside my bones.

With that, I overcome every vein of theological dissonance that pops up into my head.

God always speaks. Hope is always alive and well. I stand in the love of God and run with joy set before me.

Be encouraged! You're a blood-bought, Spirit-filled, child of God, seated in heavenly places with Christ right now. Don't let any form of theological dissonance silence your mouth from speaking the living Word of God over yourself and those around you.

Open your heart. Unlock your ears. "[Build] yourselves up in your most holy faith and praying in the Holy Spirit" (Jude 20). "Fan into flame the gift of God, which is in you" (2 Timothy 1:6). Cling to this promise from Isaiah 40:31:

Even youths grow tired and weary,
 and young men stumble and fall;

but those who hope in the LORD
 will renew their strength.
They will soar on wings like eagles;
 they will run and not grow weary,
 they will walk and not be faint.

The invitation isn't to figure everything out. It's to come close. Stay near. Stop demanding answers from God. When you do, you'll find that even the silence speaks. Even the mystery forms you. And even when you don't have the words, you are being held by the One who is the Word everlasting.

3 WAYS TO OVERCOME PROPHETIC BARRIERS

1. Relational Trust Is Everything

Trusting God isn't just about hearing His voice. It's about trusting His heart even when you don't hear Him. No child only trusts his dad when he can hear his voice. There's a deeper knowing than what comes from hearing. This is why it's so important to have the written Word deep in the wells of your soul. It's a reservoir in times of divine silence. As we read previously in Amos 3:7, "Surely the Sovereign LORD does nothing without revealing his plan to his servants the prophets."

God is always in control, but He doesn't always take control. He lets us walk. He lets us discover. He lets us seek. He knows that seeking is often better than finding. Think about it this way: Parents don't hide Easter eggs "from" their kids. They hide Easter eggs "for" their kids. Why? Because searching is a sacred part of life. Seeking God is seeking His voice, His will, His face, His desire, His leading, His answer, His nature, and more.

Why would we punish ourselves by resenting a God who chooses to not reveal a warning or a clue when He is constantly revealing so much more? Then again, what if He did speak and did warn, but you were too busy to sense the whisper? This is why *pneumatikos*, being spiritually awake, matters. It's not about knowing everything but being fully alive to His whisper.

This is what Paul meant when he told Timothy, "Fan into flame the gift of God, which is in you" (2 Timothy 1:6). The apostle didn't say, "Wait until you understand everything." He wanted Timothy to stir it up now. Activate it now. Don't let it go dormant just because you don't have all the answers.

When we press through dissonance, trusting the Spirit-led relationship, we don't lose faith. We find fire. And that fire spreads, not because we shouted louder but because we trusted deeper.

2. Understanding New Testament Prophecy

Even though I wasn't skiing, I've stood at the base of Crested Butte's North Face Glades, looking up at a run marked by double black diamonds. It's ridiculous. Just looking at it screams, "Elite Experts Only! Clumsy Dumpty, stay away!"

We laugh, but that's exactly how most people think of the prophetic gifts. When you say the word *prophet*, they picture Elijah calling fire down from heaven or Isaiah prophesying about a virgin giving birth centuries before Jesus arrived. They think of thunder, visions, warnings, and world-shifting pronouncements. In other words, it's all black-diamond level stuff.

And in the Old Testament, it often was that way. Prophets stood alone in the gap. Their words were binding, and their revelation had to be perfect. If they missed the mark, they weren't just rebuked. They were stoned.

That's why so many modern believers stay silent. Somewhere deep down, they think, *Unless I'm Elijah or Isaiah, I shouldn't even try. I don't want God to kill me!* But that's not how New Testament prophecy works.

Jesus and the Woman at the Well

Let's explore one of the most beautiful prophetic encounters in the Bible, one that bridges both the awe and accessibility of God's voice.

In John 4, Jesus is tired. The disciples go into town for lunch while He sits by a well, which is the very same setting where Isaac's servant once met Rebekah (Genesis 24) and Jacob met Rachel (Genesis 29). In Jewish tradition, wells weren't just about water. They were about meeting. They were a significant reminder of patriarchal covenant, provision, and fulfillment.

So when Jesus starts a conversation with a Samaritan woman at this well, He's doing more than asking for a drink. He's doing something prophetic. He had to go there. The Father sent Him there.

Jesus gives this woman prophetic words of knowledge, things He couldn't know without the Father revealing them by the Spirit. She's had five husbands. This does not necessarily point to adultery on her part. More likely, these men left her for any number of reasons, including the inability to fulfill their desires for children or even death. We don't know the exact reasons from Scripture, but we do know that five different men married her. That's amazing in that culture. She was special. But she lost all five somehow. She was broken.

Jesus didn't tell this Samaritan woman to go leave her life of sin. This is one indication that she was probably in her fifties or sixties and was living with a brother or possibly her son. Regardless, Jesus prophesied a word of knowledge. No accusations. No shame. Just revelation with precision. The kind that makes her whisper, "Sir, I perceive that you are a prophet" (John 4:19 ESV).

Moments later, the woman runs back into town shouting, "Come, see a man who told me everything I ever did. Could this be the Messiah?" (John 4:29) And all the people come out to see Him.

> Many of the Samaritans from that town believed in him because of the woman's testimony … And because of his words many more became believers. They said to the woman, "We no longer believe just because of what you said; now we have heard for ourselves, and we know that this man really is the Savior of the world." (John 4:39, 41–42)

Notice that this encounter is nothing like Old Testament prophecy. This is more like my encounter with Sky at Haywire and hundreds of others I've had all over the world. Jesus didn't make water start pouring out of the well. He didn't make a mountain fall. He didn't call down fire or write the woman's name in the sky. Instead, He revealed the Father's heart through a prophetic word of knowledge to one broken person, and it changed an entire town.

That's what New Testament prophecy is about: access to God's heart and building people up. You don't have to be one of the elites, and you don't have to have superhero powers. Paul wrote, "Follow the way of love and eagerly desire gifts of the Spirit, especially prophecy" (1 Corinthians 14:1). Not especially miracles. Not especially tongues. Not especially evangelism.

"Especially prophecy." Why? Because "the one who prophesies speaks to people for their strengthening, encouraging and comfort" (1 Corinthians 14:3).

The Framework That Brings Freedom

Again, the fourfold framework applies powerfully.

- **Diversities of gifts**—Different prophetic abilities are available to all believers.

- **Differences of ministries**—Some operate in prayer closets, others in restaurants, and others in more public settings.

- **Diversities of activities**—Some receive gentle impressions, while others get bold declarations.

- **Manifestations of the Spirit**—All the differences reveal God's presence and heart.

This framework explains why prophetic experiences vary so widely. A word of knowledge for Sky came during a family dinner (gift + ministry + activity + manifestation). In our services at Anchor, the same gift manifested through different preparation and different delivery but the same Spirit. (I'll share more on that in a moment.)

Understanding New Testament Community

There's a huge difference between the office of the prophet (Ephesians 4) and the gift of prophecy for the New Testament church community (1 Corinthians 12–14).

I would like every one of you to speak in tongues, but I would
rather have you prophesy. The one who prophesies is greater than
the one who speaks in tongues, unless someone interprets, so that
the church may be edified. (1 Corinthians 14:5)

I will pour out my Spirit on all people.
    Your sons and daughters will prophesy.
(Joel 2:28; cf. Acts 2:17)

I wish that all the LORD's people were prophets and that the LORD
would put his Spirit on them! (Numbers 11:29)

God isn't lowering the bar. He's opening the door to everyone who
has the Spirit living in them. We all have our own areas of influence,
and people need to know the voice of God and receive the blessings
that come from the insight gifts.

So many people think, *I wish I could get a word from the pastor on a
Sunday morning in front of the whole room.* This is why God wants all of
His sons and daughters to prophesy. He wants the blessing to come
not only from stages but also be activated in community.

This is superbloom. This is the soil of the church community being
awakened and people receiving strength, courage, and comfort by the
Spirit through ordinary people like us.

Prophecy is for the old men with robes and scrolls *and* the woman at
the well. It's also for

- the server at Haywire.

- the granddaughter who's harming herself and can't find joy.

- the entrepreneur facing the fiftieth barrier in advancement.

- the empty-nest couple whose newfound freedom is actually
  lonely.

- the mom who hears something for her child.

- the servant who listens and dares to speak.

And what about when people get it wrong? Paul writes, "For we know in part and we prophesy in part" (1 Corinthians 13:9) and "Do not treat prophecies with contempt but test them all; hold on to what is good" (1 Thessalonians 5:20–21). We don't worship prophecy, and we don't throw it out when it's partial. We always weigh it.

3. Discernment: Learning to Distinguish the Spirits

This issue goes back all the way to the Garden of Eden. God created us to know Him, be loved by Him, and delight in His glory forever. However, He also knew, even before we fell, we would be so weak that He would have to become flesh and die to save us. He created us to trust Him while He was fully present in the Garden of Eden. But even in that perfect atmosphere, we lacked the ability to discern the real meaning of the knowledge of good and evil. We couldn't even discern the serpent as evil and God as good.

That was before the fall of man and before we had a sin nature. How much more does God know that in the twenty-first century, human beings need some serious help to discern spiritual things and know Him so well that we can distinguish good and evil?

The Dullness of the Disciples

The disciples struggled with this, even though they were right there with Jesus. They saw how He heard the Father, they heard Him pray, and they watched Him yield. They even witnessed Him in His glorified body, and still they missed huge spiritual clues.

- In Matthew 16:6, Jesus warns, "Beware of the yeast of the Pharisees and Sadducees" (NLT). The disciples think He's talking about bread. He rebukes them: "Do you still not understand?" (v. 9)

- In Mark 4:40, after calming the storm, Jesus asks, "Why are you so afraid? Do you still have no faith?"

- In Luke 24:25, on the road to Emmaus, Jesus says, "How foolish you are, and how slow to believe all that the prophets have spoken!"

- In Matthew 26:40, in the Garden of Gethsemane, Jesus asks Peter, "Couldn't you men keep watch with me for one hour?"

- In John 14:9, Jesus asks Philip, "Don't you know me, Philip, even after I have been among you such a long time?"

- In Mark 8:18, Jesus asks, "Do you have eyes but fail to see, and ears but fail to hear?"

These weren't harsh rejections. They were invitations to grow. Over and over again, Jesus did more than perform miracles. He trained their senses.

The Road to Emmaus: Eyes Opened, Hearts Burning

Nowhere is this clearer than in Luke 24. Two disciples walk seven miles with Jesus after the resurrection and don't even recognize Him. Why? Because Jesus was doing spiritual rehab. He was reconditioning their senses. He was teaching them to hear before they saw, opening the Scriptures before opening their eyes.

Luke 24:31 says, "Then their eyes were opened and they recognized him, and he disappeared from their sight." This wasn't a failure of intellect. It was a lack of spiritual sensitivity.

But notice what they say after Jesus vanishes: "Were not our hearts burning within us while he talked with us on the road and opened the Scriptures to us?" (v. 32) They didn't see Him first. They felt Him first. This is the moment when spiritual maturity begins. When you start training yourself to sense God in the unseen, the "eyes of the heart" start to open.

WORDS OF KNOWLEDGE AND WISDOM

In the broader category of insight gifts, prophecy is often accompanied by words of knowledge and words of wisdom. These gifts are deeply scriptural, incredibly practical, and completely accessible.

Word of Knowledge

This is a supernatural insight into something you could not have known otherwise. It often includes a detail, such as a name, a condition, a secret pain, or a recent event, that unlocks faith in the hearer.

Jesus exercised this gift constantly.

- With Nathanael: "I saw you while you were still under the fig tree" (John 1:48).

- With the woman at the well: "You have had five husbands" (John 4:17).

- With Sky: He knew she was fulfilling the role of a matriarch, carrying family burdens.

It's not guessing. It's not magic. It's the Spirit whispering a detail that softens a heart for God to enter.

Word of Wisdom

This is a Spirit-led solution or direction rooted in God's perspective. It often comes during moments of tension, decision, or confrontation. Biblically, wisdom always begins with the fear of the Lord (see Proverbs 9:10). It isn't cleverness or assessing a situation. It's submission to heaven's mind and seeing the path forward.

Prophetic Ministry Sunday Morning

The week after I taught on these gifts, so many overwhelming testimonies came in, and I'm going to share some of them with you here. But first, it's important to note that I've seen and experienced the gifts of prophecy, words of knowledge, and words of wisdom happen in a room where people were left more suspicious than encouraged. Our social media-driven, technology-obsessed world makes it so easy to access information about people. When I preached, I wanted the Lord to do something that wouldn't be suspicious at all. I wanted Him to be glorified.

This is very risky for a pastor, especially a pastor like me. I'm in the lobby after all four services with thousands of people a week. I'm in restaurants, homes, workplaces, and golf courses with even more people. I didn't want anyone thinking, *He already knew that about them, so that's not a prophetic word.*

So, when I was in prayer four hours before the 8:30 Father's Day Service, I asked the Lord, "What do You have for the fathers or men today?" I started to see the room through the eyes of my heart, and the Lord began to show me specific men and give me very specific words for them.

I always build my own slides for ProPresenter. For point one, this was on the screen: "Hebrews 13:5–6 (1S: L/WS/Family)." That stood for first service, left/white shirt/family. Then I shared a written, very specific prophetic word for a man with a white shirt on the left side with his family. I wrote it hours before the service.

The Lord had words like this for fourteen different men, each with specific details in each service. I submitted three different presentations to the media team and labeled them "8:30 Svc," "10:00 Svc," and "11:45 Svc." Each point had different cues for specific people. I also printed out the specific words and taped them in the back of my Bible. After the service, I gave the written copy to the couples if they wanted it.

Now, let's dive into those testimonies.

The Purple Shirt Worship Leaders

"James 1:5-7 (1S: Couples/LS-P&LB)." That stood for first service/couples/left/purple & light blue shirt. As soon as the slide went up, everyone in the room looked over to my left and laughed because it was so specific. There were literally two couples sitting right beside each other, and one husband had on a light blue shirt while the other was right beside him with a purple shirt.

I had no idea who these people were, but I sensed the Lord saying that there was going to be a breakthrough of "reasonable skepticism" and that they needed to start singing together in their quiet time. It was rooted in James 1:5–7.

The next day, one of the men messaged my wife:

Hi Mrs. Jenkins, my wife and I got a prophetic word at the 8:30 a.m. service. It was the light blue/purple shirt couple one. It couldn't have been more accurate for us. We both sing, we are both musicians, and for some reason we haven't sung together in the last few months. And the part about skepticism was something we had talked about together just yesterday. God is so good. We were wondering if you could send us a picture of it? We were stunned in the moment because of how much we needed this word and would love to see it again.

The Engagement Ring Revelation (Word of Knowledge)

"10S/Young couple, RS, WS." I began giving them a word about their relationship, then asked, "Are y'all married?" They shook their heads no. I said, "Well, you're gonna be. If you like it, you better put a ring on it." I was embarrassed because they weren't married, so I was just being humorous about it. Afterward, I felt so awkward and was repeating to myself, "Never do that again."

After the service, the young man approached me in front of four other men and said, "Pastor Jeff, I was the one you asked if we were married. Pastor, I bought an engagement ring last week, and I'm proposing this week." The young woman later messaged me on Instagram: "We felt the presence of the Lord more than ever, and to hear such a moving message was truly beautiful and inspiring in our relationship."

The Colombian Preacher

"HS/RS." (Hispanic man/Right Side). A young man immediately stood up. The word included, "The Lord has given you an ability to teach and lead people into simple truths. Do not despise the day of small beginnings."

Three days later, his neighbor messaged me: "You gave him a word that deeply moved him, and he couldn't wait to tell me. Thanks for stepping out in faith."

The Yellow and Blue Miracle

"3S/Couple Y&B." This one still amazes me. In the 11:45 service, I had a word of wisdom rooted in James 1:5–7 written out for a married couple wearing yellow and blue. In the packed service, only one couple wore those colors: Pat and Rita on the back row. I shared wisdom about rest, taking vacation, their business, and next trip. After service, Pat said they had no trip planned "but we do now." Rita later explained that she'd changed from black to yellow that morning, and when Pat asked her about shirt colors, she said "Blue." It seems that the Lord was encouraging them to get away, rest and even used those clothing choices to help them and others know with certainty that He still speaks.

Move or Stay (Prophecy, Word of Knowledge, Word of Wisdom)

"Second service, middle, white shirt." I received a word about not rushing major decisions, and even though they think there are only two options on the table, many more are there.

The wife later messaged me:

> Friday night, we debated moving back to my hometown or to another state. Sunday morning, my husband couldn't decide what to wear and said "Should I wear this white shirt? I feel like I've worn it a lot." When you started giving words, I thought, *How cool would it be if the Lord had a word for us.* Then you pointed to him and spoke words that sounded like you'd heard our conversation.

It broke a barrier we didn't know existed and showed us we aren't forgotten.

There were fourteen words altogether. It was a unique day at Anchor Church.

What Made These Words Authentic?

Several things protected these prophetic moments from manipulation:

1. **Advance Preparation**—I wrote down everything hours before the services started and taped the words in my Bible.

2. **Specific Details**—The clothing, seating, and circumstances couldn't be guessed.

3. **Humble Delivery**—I always presented the words as "what I believe the Lord is saying."

4. **Biblical Foundation**—Every word aligned with Scripture and God's character.

5. **Encouraging Purpose**—All words strengthened, encouraged, and comforted.

6. **External Confirmation**—There were multiple witnesses and follow-up testimonies.

The goal was never to impress people with my "spiritual abilities" but to serve them with God's heart.

Prophecy is born in intimacy, not performance.

GETTING STARTED: POSITIONING YOURSELF FOR PROPHETIC MINISTRY

If you've read this far and thought, *I wish I could hear God like that,* here are five practical steps to position yourself for the insight gifts.

1. Develop Daily Intimacy

Every prophetic word I've shared came during regular prayer time, not while trying to "get a word" for someone. Prophecy is born in intimacy, not performance. This is my daily rhythm:

- Start with worship and Scripture.

- It's 100 percent faith. You only "know" in relationship with Him.

- Journal what you sense the Spirit saying.

- Ask God to give you His heart for others.

- Pay attention to impressions during prayer.

2. Learn to Test Everything

Not every impression is from God. Develop discernment by

- testing impressions against Scripture.

- looking for the fruit of the Spirit (love, joy, peace, and so on).

- asking, "Does this strengthen, encourage, or comfort?"

- getting input from mature believers.

3. Start Small and Safe

Practice with close friends who give you permission to share encouraging impressions in low-pressure settings. Always say, "This is what I sense," not "Thus says the Lord." And be willing to be wrong without being devastated or stoned to death.

4. Focus on Building Others Up

Remember 1 Corinthians 14:3: Prophecy is for "strengthening, encouraging and comfort." If what you're sensing doesn't build people up, it's probably not prophetic ministry.

5. Study How Jesus Did It

Look at Jesus' prophetic encounters:

- The woman at the well (John 4)

- Nathanael under the fig tree (John 1)

- The rich young ruler (Mark 10)

Notice how He combined supernatural insight with genuine love and practical wisdom.

TRAINING YOUR SPIRITUAL SENSES

Hebrews 5:14 says, "But solid food is for the mature, who by constant use have trained themselves to distinguish good from evil." The Greek word translated "trained" here is *gumnazō*, from which we get the word gymnasium. And the word for "senses" is *aisthētērion*, meaning organs of perception, or spiritual discernment faculties developed through repeated, practiced use.

This isn't about your five natural senses. It is possible to get really weird with this and spend hours trying to "smell" heaven. If you spend too much time there, you'll end up disconnected from the head (Jesus), and you'll start rooting your spirituality in your sensory experiences (see Colossians 2:19).

It's true that God can use your natural senses to speak to you. I'll talk more about this in the next chapter on the gift of healings. Sometimes He lets us know things spiritually by giving us promptings in our feelings, body, or senses. I've experienced this many times.

However, discernment training goes much deeper. It's the internal ability to recognize the presence of God, the character of God, the will of God, the wisdom of God, the encouragement of God, and the way of God, and to sense what spirit is at work at all times. The purpose is to grow up in Him and discern truth from error, even when it's subtle.

This level of discernment doesn't come through head knowledge. It comes through a life of discipline, mature submission, and active participation with the Holy Spirit. It requires

- paying attention to patterns and ways.

- testing what you sense against Scripture.

- staying humble and correctable.

- choosing relationship over suspicion.

This kind of maturity won't happen instantly. It's trained over time.

You won't always get it right, but God is looking for participation, not perfection. Paul writes,

> The person without the Spirit does not accept the things that come from the Spirit of God but considers them foolishness, and cannot understand them because they are discerned only through the Spirit. The person with the Spirit makes judgments about all things. (1 Corinthians 2:14–15)

Discernment is for the growing, not the elite. The more you train, the more tuned-in you become. You hear the Spirit, and you begin to sense His nudges, recognize His fingerprints, and obey Him with greater confidence.

THE EVERYDAY PROPHETIC LIFE

I want you to understand that prophetic ministry isn't about becoming a spiritual superstar. No, it's about becoming someone who consistently hears God's heart for others and has the courage to share it in love.

- It's Sky at Haywire receiving exactly what she needed to hear.

- It's the dating couple getting confirmation about their future.

- It's the Colombian man being affirmed in his calling.

- It's Pat and Rita getting a business strategy rooted in rest.

- It's the couple debating two moves and discovering God has more.

- It's the worship-leading couple getting breakthrough in "sing more."

It's countless more moments where heaven touches earth through ordinary people who've learned to listen.

You don't need a title or a platform. You need a relationship with God and love for people. The same Spirit who gave me words for strangers in a restaurant wants to speak through you to encourage someone in your office, your neighborhood, or your family.

If you're filled with the Spirit, then yes, you're already qualified. Are you willing to step out of your comfort zone into the beautiful risk of partnering with God's voice?

WHERE SILENCE BECOMES SACRED

Let me close this chapter where we started: with the mystery of God's timing and the tension of theological dissonance. You are not meant to live passively or numb. You are meant to live discerning, alert, and alive in the Spirit. God is raising up believers who know His voice, walk by His whisper, and move with holy confidence, not because they're prophets but because they're mature.

But you're also not meant to live under the pressure of having to hear God about *everything*. Sometimes the greatest act of faith is trusting God's heart when you can't hear His voice. Sometimes the most prophetic thing you can do is rest in His sovereignty when you don't have supernatural insight.

Both the words and the silence are sacred. Both the revelations and the mysteries are holy. Both the times when heaven feels close and the seasons when it feels distant are opportunities to know God more deeply.

So whether you're sitting in a restaurant receiving an impression about your waitress or sitting in the pitch-dark piney woods of North Louisiana wondering if your son is alive, remember this: God is with you. He sees you. He knows your need. And sometimes the most profound word He speaks is the one that echoes in the silence of your surrendered heart: *I am enough*.

The insight gifts reveal the heart. The impact gifts reveal the hand. When those two come together, the kingdom breaks through in undeniable power.

Let's go there next.

CHAPTER 8 STUDY GUIDE

But the one who prophesies speaks to people for their
strengthening, encouraging, and comfort.

—1 Corinthians 14:3

REVIEW

Theological dissonance happens as we wonder why we sometimes hear God clearly for others but experience silence about our own situations. Understanding that "we know in part and prophesy in part" frees us from the pressure of perfection and opens the door to humble service rather than spiritual performance.

The gifts of prophecy, words of knowledge, and words of wisdom reveal God's heart through supernatural insight that strengthens, encourages, and comforts others. Unlike Old Testament prophecy reserved for select prophets, New Testament prophecy is accessible to all believers. It functions within the fourfold framework of different gifts, different ministries, different activities, and different manifestations of the same Spirit.

Words of knowledge reveal details we couldn't naturally know. Words of wisdom provide Spirit-led solutions and direction. Prophecy speaks God's heart for building up the body. These insight gifts work through ordinary believers in everyday moments and places, anywhere people yield to the Spirit's promptings.

Prophetic ministry flows from relational trust and from training our spiritual senses through constant use. Even in seasons of divine silence, God is forming us and drawing us deeper into relationship with Him—the foundation from which all prophetic ministry flows.

KEY SCRIPTURES

For we know in part and we prophesy in part. (1 Corinthians 13:9)

I would like every one of you to speak in tongues, but I would rather have you prophesy. The one who prophesies is greater than the one who speaks in tongues, unless someone interprets, so that the church may be edified. (1 Corinthians 14:5)

Do not treat prophecies with contempt but test them all; hold on to what is good. (1 Thessalonians 5:20–21)

But solid food is for the mature, who by constant use have trained themselves to distinguish good from evil. (Hebrews 5:14)

GROUP DISCUSSION

1. How can believers support each other through the painful tension of hearing God clearly for others but feeling silence about our own crises? What responses help versus hurt when someone shares this struggle?

2. How does recognizing the shift from Old Testament to New Testament prophecy change what we should expect from each other in everyday life? In what ways does this accessibility bring unity rather than competition?

3. What principles need to be more widely taught about how prophetic words should be prepared, delivered, and received? What safeguards protect against manipulation?

4. How can we help each other distinguish between our thoughts, God's voice, and other influences? What pat-

terns or practices could we share that have helped us recognize the Spirit's promptings?

5.   How could our group create a safe environment to practice prophetic gifts with permission, grace for mistakes, and biblical accountability?

PERSONAL REFLECTION

1.   How would you describe your current level of trust in God's heart, even when you can't hear His voice clearly?

2.   Have you been waiting for Old Testament prophetic experiences? What would change if you started expecting God to speak through ordinary, everyday encounters?

3.   What practices help you discern God's voice? Where do you need more development?

4.   Which step of positioning yourself for prophetic ministry represents your biggest growth opportunity? What specific action could you take this week to develop greater sensitivity to God's voice for others?

PRAYER

Father God, thank You for opening the door to prophetic ministry for all believers through the Holy Spirit. Teach us to recognize Your voice with clarity while resting in Your sovereignty during seasons of silence. When theological dissonance tempts us to doubt, remind us that You are enough.

Help us trust Your heart in every situation. Train our spiritual senses to distinguish good from evil and give us courage to partner with Your voice through simple obedience in restaurants, workplaces, homes, and wherever we go. Let every word we speak strengthen, encourage, and comfort others. In Jesus' name, Amen.

9

WHEN GOD WORKS

*The Healings, The Miracles,
The Mighty Hand*

A portent [miracle], therefore, happens not contrary to nature, but contrary to what we know as nature."

—Augustine of Hippo, *City of God*

Jesus Christ is the same yesterday and today and forever.

—Hebrews 13:8

Truly, truly, I say to you, whoever believes in me will also do the works that I do…

—John 14:12

"CAN YOU MEET me at Del Frisco's at noon? I have something hard to share with you and something really hard to share with you." That was the text I received from my dear friend Joel Stockstill on June 30, 2023. It was cryptic, but I knew Joel well enough to know he wasn't playing games. I made my way there, not knowing that lunch would feel more like holy ground.

The hard news wasn't that bad. The really hard news was this: "Jeff, I just found out this morning from Dad's doctor that Dad only has thirty days to live."

I don't remember what I ate.

I do remember the lump in my throat and the stillness that settled over the table like a thick cloud of glory and sorrow all at once. Only Joel and one of his brothers knew at the time. It was sacred space, the kind of moment where you feel the weight of generational mantle and personal grief all at once.

I've already mentioned Joel's dad, Larry, a few times in this book, but I need to tell you more. For the first twenty years of my life, I never set foot in a Spirit-filled or charismatic church. I was raised in Church of Christ congregations where the Word was central, but we didn't talk about gifts, miracles, or prophecy. We loved the Bible, but we didn't expect God to speak through it in real time. We sang without instruments and studied the Gospels like sacred maps, but we didn't talk about the Holy Spirit leading us in power.

Then, in the summer of 1994, I was a sophomore at LSU, and a friend convinced me to visit a church called Bethany World Prayer Center in Baker, Louisiana. It was a Wednesday night service called "Peak of the Week." We parked in the back and walked through a dark, crowded parking lot toward a 6,000-seat sanctuary with about 2,500 hungry believers packed in near the front. The atmosphere was thick with worship, expectation, and something I couldn't name at the time. I just knew it was *alive*.

That night, I watched Larry Stockstill lead worship, pray over the crowd, take the offering, preach the Word, and call people to the altar. He did it all with a grace and flow I had never seen before. It was like watching a spiritual symphony led by one conductor who wasn't trying to perform but simply obey.

For the next several years, I attended Bethany's midweek and Saturday night services whenever I could. I would take notes on Larry's sermons, rewrite them in my own words, and teach them to college students on campus.

I was captivated by the integrity of his preaching and the clarity of his leadership. Through him, I saw the Spirit move. Now, I'll admit that there were some very weird, crazy things that happened; I blame that on mixing Cajuns with the Holy Spirit. But from Larry himself, there was zero showmanship. I saw only Spirit-filled shepherding. And I never forgot it.

A PROPHETIC DREAM

Fast forward to November 4, 2010. At 2:30 in the morning, I woke up from one of the five most vivid prophetic dreams of my life. I wrote every detail down and sent it to a mentor of mine. "Sit on it," he told me. "Wait and watch. When it's time, you'll know."

Here are the bullet points from the dream:

- I was in Baton Rouge with Sarah.

- I was hopping from construction site to construction site.

- I landed back at our car and asked Sarah, "What if we planted a church here?"

- Then I arrived at a northeast site, and it was Larry Stockstill's church.

- I had a clear impression to go to his house and tell him, "God's calling me to serve the vision He just revealed to you. That vision is to multiply over one million churches worldwide, and I'm here to serve it."

Not your average pizza-and-too-much-coffee dream, that's for sure. But I obeyed. I held on to it, prayed into it, and waited.

On March 12, 2015 (four years, four months, and eight days later), a friend invited me to lunch, and I accepted. Sarah and I had just moved to McKinney, Texas, to plant Anchor Church. A few moments after I arrived at the restaurant, Joel Stockstill sat down at the table. I knew who he was, but we'd never met.

Halfway through that lunch, I knew it was time. I told him the dream, word for word. Joel sat still. He didn't roll his eyes or politely nod. He leaned in. He listened. Then he said, "You need to meet my dad." A few days later, I did. That one dream led to a connection that changed the trajectory of my life and ministry.

I didn't know when I had that dream in 2010 that back in 2001, Larry Stockstill had founded a church-planting organization called the Global 12 Project (later renamed Surge). He had gathered apostolic leaders in Switzerland, divided the world into twelve regions with appointed Regional Directors, and launched a strategy built on empowering native workers—pastors who speak the language, understand the culture, and live among their own people. This approach has led to exponential growth and thousands of churches planted worldwide.

I didn't even know that organization existed when I had my dream, but the vision matched Surge's global mission perfectly: to plant one million churches around the world. Sometimes the Spirit speaks before we even know what He's speaking to. In 2020, Larry transitioned the Executive Director role to Joel, and the vision continues into a new era of what God is doing globally.

Since then, I've participated in Larry's Pastor's University training and have brought several of my pastoral staff through his ministry training. I have been in numerous board meetings with him, and I have received dozens of prophetic ministry moments that were so powerful in my life. Seriously, God has changed my whole prayer life and faith through these men. They are family to me, and our friendship is so dear to my heart.

So when Joel told me Larry had thirty days to live, it wasn't just grief I felt. It was covenant. It was spiritual family. It was legacy. And what followed over the next six months was nothing short of a miracle.

LARRY'S MIRACLE HEALING

Larry dropped from 190 pounds to 140 pounds as three blood diseases tormented his body. He had polycythemia vera, myelofibrosis, and leukemia. He was on a walker for four months as his body was too weak to walk unassisted. He came to McKinney, Texas, for a blood treatment, and we had lunch afterward. I believed it would be the last time I saw him alive.

The entire lunch, he prophesied over me and Anchor Church. He asked about me, my wife, and each of my kids. He never lost his focus. He never stopped being a spiritual father. When he got up to get some pudding, he shuffled so slowly that I almost felt compelled to carry him. But it was clear: Larry was walking out his miracle healing by faith.

One day, having had transfusions two days a week all day for several months, his doctor said, "You need to call hospice. We are just giving you blood, and you are not making your own." He reluctantly agreed to give Larry one more month of blood.

Larry should have collapsed. But the Spirit of the Lord empowered him to keep worshipping. As Larry sat through most conversations just to conserve energy, the Lord gave his spirit grace to never fade. Many of us wept with him when he taught, prophesied and prayed over us and could barely lift his hands. The Lord graced him to keep on praying and keep on praising. He also kept on fathering.

One month later, when his son moved to Alabama, the Lord spoke to Larry to leave his walker at home and drive to Huntsville with his son. Like the ten lepers going to the priest before their healing, Larry obeyed. That evening, his healing began. He not only didn't need the walker, but he also walked everywhere and helped to unload the trailer. When he returned home, he looked so good that his son, Jonathan, asked him to preach the next Sunday (the first time in seven months). Within two more months, his hemoglobin had risen from 3.5 (normal is 14-15) to over 7. The doctor said that he needed no more transfusions. That was two years ago, and he has not had a blood transfusion since that time. His hemoglobin was recently tested at 14.9, perfectly normal. He is travelling overseas, preaching up to eight times on a weekend, and giving God all the glory!

Over the course of a few short weeks, the healing came. Larry's strength returned. His voice returned. His weight returned. He danced in worship again. By December 2024, Larry was preaching again. In January 2025, he preached in every service at Anchor Church. Larry ministered that morning for five hours straight, often giving prophetic words to our staff during the breaks between services and after the service.

What I witnessed wasn't hype or exaggeration or platform energy. It was the fruit of a man of sincere faith, shaped by decades of devotion, living out a miracle before our eyes. Larry looked death in the face and kept his eyes on Jesus. He didn't fake it. He didn't perform. He trusted.

People criticize large churches, and I get it. There's mess in every movement. But I know Larry, and his obedience has led to over 40,000 churches being planted around the world. He has raised spiritual sons who lead some of the largest and healthiest churches in the country.

Larry's message at Anchor was called "Three Steps Forward," and it was based on Joshua chapters 3–4. He mapped out a beautiful testimony of how he trusted and walked by faith when he couldn't see how to stand. But not everyone loved the message.

THEOLOGICAL DISSONANCE POPS UP AGAIN

Just days after Larry's message, I got a message from a man I know well. He and his wife had lost their baby girl to cancer less than eighteen months before. When he heard Larry share about his healing, the man said he couldn't take it.

In a pretty clear way, I knew he wasn't going to be talked into coming back. He wasn't angry at Larry. He was angry at the gap. This man had done all the same things. Prayed. Believed. Worshipped. And still, he buried his daughter.

That's where we must go next. Healing and miracles are not a formula. They're not a reward for effort or proof of greater faith. They're the mystery of God's mighty hand.

I'm going to teach on the gift of healings and the working of miracles later in this chapter. I'm going to map out the healthiest ways I know to operate in these gifts and how to do so with *pneumatikos* (spiritual maturity). But before we go there, I want to address the huge tension that we all have about this subject.

One family sees a miracle while another buries a child. In those moments, faith can start to feel like a loaded word. Not a lifeline but a landmine. It's like getting a word for Sky but not getting a word for my son. The main difference with these impact gifts of healings and miracles is not revelation of a word but the death of a loved one.

Why does one story end in healing and another in heartbreak? Why does faith feel like it works sometimes, but other times it doesn't? I've walked with people on both sides of that equation. Some shouted declarations of faith while hooked up to IVs. Others refused to pray at all because they didn't want to be disappointed.

And in the middle is an aching confusion nobody really wants to talk about.

Four Reasons We Struggle

Let's walk through each of these reasons, not like a seminary class but as a conversation. These aren't theories; they're real tensions, felt by real people trying to hold onto real hope.

1. We Misunderstand God's Will

There's an idea floating around (sometimes spoken, sometimes just assumed) that if it's God's will, you won't suffer. Or if you have enough faith, you won't be sick.

But the Bible doesn't tell that story. (I realize that might be shocking, but stay with me.) Take Paul, the apostle, missionary, and writer of much of the New Testament. He had a "thorn in the flesh" (2 Corinthians 12:7). Scholars debate whether it was a physical issue, demonic opposition, or maybe something emotional. Whatever it was, Paul begged God to take it away. Not once. Not twice. Three times.

God said no. Why? Because Paul lacked faith? Because he was being punished? Neither. God wanted to display a greater power: sustaining grace. He told Paul, "My grace is sufficient for you, for my power is made perfect in weakness" (2 Corinthians 12:9). That doesn't sell books. But it saves souls. God's will isn't always painless, but it's always purposeful.

One thing that's true about every person I've read about in the Gospels who operated in the full power of the Holy Spirit and had the highest levels of faith is this: They all suffered greatly. In fact, except for John, they all died in the most horrendous ways. John survived being boiled in oil.

We assume God's goodness always looks like physical healing right now. Yes, the will of God for your life is divine health. He wants your life to prosper as your soul prospers. However, that prosperity is so much bigger than the absence of sickness and financial overflow.

2. We Misplace the Purpose of Faith

We treat faith like a tool to get what we want, not a trust that shapes who we become. Nowhere is that tension clearer than in John 11 in the story of Lazarus.

Jesus hears His friend is sick in Bethany. But instead of rushing, He waits two days before heading toward the village. In that waiting, Lazarus dies.

When Jesus finally arrives, Lazarus's sister Martha runs to meet Him: "Lord … if you had been here, my brother would not have died" (v. 21). It's grief wrapped in theology.

Jesus replies, "Your brother will rise again" (v. 23).

Martha affirms what she knows: "I know he will rise again in the resurrection at the last day" (v. 24). She's standing in front of Jesus and slightly mocking Him for not temporarily healing her brother.

But Jesus interrupts her: "I am the resurrection and the life" (v. 25). He doesn't say, "I'll perform a resurrection" and describe what He will do. Instead, He declares who He is. This is the moment where faith is redefined, not as a belief for an outcome but as a relationship with a Person. He is the goal, not the healing or the miracle.

Jesus approaches the tomb, and something stirs in Him: "He was deeply moved in spirit and troubled.… Jesus wept" (v. 33, 35). The Greek says He snorted with indignation (*embrimaomai*), was agitated (*tarassó*), and shed tears (*dakruó*). This is a divine storm in the midst of human blindness to the Resurrection. Jesus wasn't weeping because Lazarus died. He wept because the crowd didn't recognize who was standing in front of them. The Resurrection was present, and still, they begged for a temporary fix.

Even Martha, who just affirmed belief, tries to stop Jesus from opening the tomb: "But Lord … by this time there is a bad odor, for he has been there four days" (v. 39). They were asking for a miracle; Jesus was offering eternal life. The pain He felt wasn't just for Lazarus. It was for the tragic reality that even those closest to Him misunderstood the purpose of faith.

The miracle wasn't Lazarus walking out. It was Jesus showing up, as well as His own passion that would unfold within days. Faith is knowing the One who is more than enough, even when the tomb is still sealed, even when you don't get what you want.

3. We Carry the Wounds of Unanswered Prayers

Disappointments that haven't healed and questions that were never resolved become wounds we carry. Maybe this is where you've been. Maybe this is where you are now.

You did everything right. You believed. You fasted. You asked. You gathered the elders. You anointed with oil. You declared Scripture with confidence. But the healing didn't come, and now, you can't even say the word "faith" without flinching. I can think of numerous people I've walked with who didn't see the healing, and it's painful to process their loss. Their faith has changed.

This story plays out a hundred different ways. I've lived some of those ways myself. Unanswered prayers don't always destroy belief, but they leave bruises that rarely heal in silence.

Even Jesus prayed in Gethsemane, "Father, if it is possible, let this cup pass from me" (Matthew 26:39 NASB). He was fully surrendered, yet the cup wasn't removed. If the Son of God can wrestle in prayer, so can we.

And that brings us back to the tomb.

4. We Default to Extremes

Some of us grew up in movements that taught us to deny suffering. Never confess it. Never say it out loud. Just declare your healing and act like it's done.

Others grew up in traditions that taught us to dismiss miracles. Don't ask for healing. Don't expect it. Just accept suffering as your lot and look for medical answers.

Both extremes are missing something.

- The first denies the reality of suffering. It assumes that if you say the right things, God is obligated to act.

- The second dismisses the power of God to change circumstances. It assumes that if you've got a doctor, you don't need divine help.

But faith isn't about controlling outcomes, and it's not about avoiding disappointment either. It's about trusting Jesus in the mystery.

At Lazarus' tomb, Jesus wept. He didn't weep because He was helpless. He wept because He was deeply moved (*embrimaomai*). Disturbed. Angered. Stirred. He wept for the brokenness. For the curse. For the death that still reigned over creation.

And then He shouted, "Lazarus, come out!" (John 11:43) The miracle wasn't the point. Jesus was the point. Lazarus would die again one day, but the Resurrection standing in front of that tomb would defeat death forever. That's the real miracle.

If you're holding pain in one hand and hope in the other, you're not alone. If faith feels confusing right now, that's okay. Actually, that's good. That means you're still leaning in.

Faith Isn't a Formula

Faith isn't a formula. It's not a sentence to memorize or a performance to perfect. It's a relationship.

And the resurrection isn't just a promise for later. It's a Person you can trust right now.

His name is Jesus. When you know Him, when you know not just His power but also His heart, you can walk through the valley without fear. Even if you don't get the miracle you wanted, you're still held by the miracle you need.

TESTIMONIES OF POWER & MYSTERY

I've seen too much to doubt. I've seen too much to fall into superstition or oversimplifying reality. I've seen miracles on both sides of the mystery. I've seen God heal people instantly. I've seen Him walk with others through years of pain.

The older I get, the more I realize that faith is not about clarity. It's about trust. Some of the people I trust most have walked through fire with faith still burning in their eyes. Let me introduce you to a few of them.

Joel: When Healing Waits

Joel Stockstill is one of the most faithful, fierce, and fruitful men I know. He's not just a preacher. He's a father to movements. Every week, Joel coaches a global team that actively shepherds networks of over 50,000 churches around the world. He mentors dozens of US church planters as sons in the faith. He's a prolific writer, a prophetic voice, and currently finishing his doctorate in theology.

And his kidneys have not worked at all in over thirty years. Joel undergoes full dialysis three times a week. For hours, he sits in a clinic while his blood is pumped out, filtered clean of toxins and excess fluid, and then pumped back into his body.

Joel does this every single week. He's come close to death more times than he can count.

His body has limits, but his spirit has none. He contends by faith for healing in his own body every single day. I hear it, and I'm never more refreshed than when I pray with him or his dad.

Joel doesn't stop. He doesn't shrink back. He prays for others. He fasts for others. He wars for others while his own body groans for relief. When Joel's wife got pregnant with their first child after many years of trying to conceive and multiple failed adoption attempts, it wasn't just a celebration. It was a fulfillment of years of weeping, trusting, and daring to believe again.

Some men walk by sight. Joel walks by bloodwork, weakness, and unwavering faith.

 *Even if you don't get the miracle you wanted, you're still held by the miracle you need.*

Nick: No Limbs, No Limits

Nick Vujicic is a member of our church and one of the most extraordinary men alive today. I've never met a more inspiring human. He's electric, full throttle, and limbless.

Born without arms or legs, Nick has spent his life proclaiming hope to the world. He's a husband. A father of four. A preacher. A global ambassador of the Gospel. And in 2026, his story will be shared in theaters around the world through the movie *No Limbs, No Limits*.

Nick has spoken to millions of people in dozens of countries. But what makes him remarkable goes beyond his platform. It's his posture. Nick lives with a contagious joy. He's one of the most encouraging people I've ever met. God uses him more than anyone I know to actually work miracles, and he loves to pray for others to be healed, even though he personally hasn't been.

In his closet, Nick keeps two pairs of shoes: one for running and one for dancing. He's not bitter. He doesn't punish God for unanswered prayers. He prepares for the day the healing comes. But more than that, he lives as if that day is already here.

The miracle isn't in Nick's limbs. It's in his life. Nick teaches me something every time we talk: Gratitude is a gateway to power, and faith doesn't begin when you get the answer. It begins when you trust God without one.

Mariam: When the Church Becomes the Miracle

It was the beginning of the summer, and I was tired. I canceled all of my appointments for the day and went home to rest. At 2:30, I got a text asking, "Are we still on for 3:00?"

"Yep!" I replied. Honestly, I was bummed I forgot to cancel. But God was working.

The counseling session started at 3:00 in my office. At 3:10, the police knocked on my office door and asked, "Are you Pastor Jeff?"

"Yes. What's going on?"

"Well, I hate to tell you, but one of your members was just killed in an auto accident right after 2:00 pm. We have notified the wife, and she asked us to let you know."

I didn't know this family. They were new to Anchor, and I'd never even met the wife. But I drove straight to their home and met a young Nigerian mother with three children under ten years old whose world had just collapsed.

Her name is Mariam. She was in a painful and desperate place. She needed over $20,000 to cover funeral expenses and more. When I told the church about this situation the following Sunday, I said one simple thing: "Anchor, we're going to be the miracle." They gave over $40,000.

The next week, I left for sabbatical, but our team stepped in and loved Mariam so well. Just this morning, she texted me the kind of message that humbles you to your core:

> Pastor Jeff,
>
> I'm not sure where to begin to express my heartfelt gratitude for everything you've done for me during this incredibly difficult time. Your support, kindness, and compassion have been a beacon of hope and comfort to me and my family … Your actions have demonstrated the love of Christ in a tangible way, and I'm forever grateful.

The miracle wasn't just money. It was presence. It was compassion. It was love made visible. Sometimes miracles don't show up in blinding light. They show up in Chick-fil-A cards, help with mortgage payments, hugs, play dates for the kids, wisdom, casseroles, prayer vigils, and bills paid just in time. Sometimes the miracle is *us*.

WHEN THE MIGHTY HAND MOVES

The gifts of healings and the working of miracles aren't sideshows or theological debates.

They're fingerprints. I say this because the gifts are not an ability given to you from God, like many mistakenly think. Rather, they are the Spirit himself, manifesting His presence. Go back to the framework we used in earlier chapters. The gifts are Him showing up.

Yes, God still shows up. He still moves. His heart still beats with compassion, and His power still pulses through His people.

But in order to understand these gifts, we have to go back. *Way* back.

Before there were miracles in Acts, there was a wilderness. A mountain. A name.

The Names of God

Throughout the Old Testament, God revealed Himself through His names. Each name carried a revelation. A promise. A personality trait etched into eternity.

Here are nine of the covenant names that shaped Israel's understanding of who God is:

- *Jehovah Jireh*: The Lord Will Provide (Genesis 22:14)

- *Jehovah Rapha*: The Lord Who Heals You (Exodus 15:26)

- *Jehovah Nissi*: The Lord Is My Banner / Victory (Exodus 17:15)

- *Jehovah Shalom*: The Lord Is Peace (Judges 6:24)

- *Jehovah Ra'ah*: The Lord Is My Shepherd (Psalm 23:1)

- *Jehovah Tsidkenu*: The Lord Our Righteousness (Jeremiah 23:6)

- *Jehovah Shammah*: The Lord Is There (Ezekiel 48:35)

- *Jehovah Mekoddishkem*: The Lord Who Sanctifies You (Leviticus 20:8)

- *El Gibbor*: The Mighty God (Isaiah 9:6)

These names are more than poetic titles; they were covenant revelations. When God called Himself *Jehovah Rapha*, He wasn't saying,

"Sometimes I heal." He was saying, "Healing is who I Am." When He said He was *Jehovah Jireh*, He wasn't saying, "I'll help if I can." He was saying, "Provision flows from My nature."

The people of Israel learned to trust these names. They called on them in battle, in famine, in disease, and in fear. When God showed up with water in the desert, food in the wilderness, or healing from disease, they rejoiced.

But when the miracles stopped, they forgot. They rebelled when provision felt delayed. They doubted when healing seemed distant. They loved the hand of God, but they often lost sight of His heart.

The Prophets Point to a Healing Messiah

Even in their rebellion, God kept speaking. Through the prophets, He whispered a promise: A Deliverer would come, not just to fix their problems but to restore their souls.

Isaiah 35 paints the picture:

> Then will the eyes of the blind be opened,
>> and the ears of the deaf unstopped.
> Then will the lame leap like a deer,
>> and the mute tongue shout for joy. (vv. 5–6)

Isaiah 61 expanded it:

> The Spirit of the Sovereign Lord is on me …
>> to bind up the brokenhearted,
> to proclaim freedom for the captives …
>> to comfort all who mourn. (vv. 1–2)

The expectation grew. One day, Messiah would come. And when He did, healing would follow. Restoration would rush in like a flood. Not just for the body but for the whole person.

Jesus: The Name Above Every Name

And then Jesus came.

- Born to a virgin.

- Raised in obscurity.

- Baptized in the Jordan.

- Empowered by the Spirit.

And what did Jesus do? He healed. The blind saw. The lame walked. The dead lived. The lepers were cleansed. The bleeding stopped. The demons fled.

Jesus didn't just perform miracles. He embodied the *names*.

- He was *Jehovah Rapha* who healed the sick.

- He was *Jehovah Jireh* who fed the five thousand.

- He was *Jehovah Shalom* who calmed the storm.

- He was *El Gibbor* who silenced death itself.

But His greatest name was the one given at birth: *Yeshua*. This name means 'The Lord Saves.' Every healing pointed to that. Every miracle echoed it. Jesus didn't come to show off power. He came to restore people to God. He didn't come to give us temporary relief but to offer us eternal relationship.

That's why the gifts of healings and the working of miracles are still given to the Church today. Not to impress. Not to distract. But to reveal the name. To point to Jesus. To say with action what the gospel declares in words: He is here. He is alive. He still saves.

DEFINING THE GIFTS: HEALINGS AND MIRACLES

Let's put definitions to these gifts:

Gifts of healings are Spirit-empowered moments when God brings supernatural restoration to the body, mind, or soul. Sometimes the healing is instant. Sometimes it's layered. But either way, it always reveals God's love.

Workings of miracles are supernatural suspensions of natural law to demonstrate God's authority, mercy, or mission. Red Seas part. Axe heads float. Food multiplies. Bodies rise. Darkness flees. More than phenomena, they are the movements of a living God through willing vessels.

Healings and miracles are not badges of maturity. They are not rewards for good behavior. They are gifts.

WHY DOES GOD STILL HEAL? WHY DO MIRACLES STILL HAPPEN?

Because He is still *Jehovah Rapha*. He is still *Jehovah Jireh*. He is still *Yeshua*.

Because His compassion hasn't diminished. His power hasn't weakened. His Spirit hasn't changed.

Because someone needs to know He is near. Someone needs to see the gospel with their eyes. Someone needs to feel the love of God in the marrow of their bones.

And because He loves to work through ordinary people with surrendered hearts.

Now, I know some readers might agree with every sentence so far and still say, "Yes, God still heals, but He doesn't do it through people anymore." That's the heart of cessationism: the belief that while God can do miracles, He no longer empowers believers with the gifts of the Spirit to do them.

In this view, miracles are sovereign interruptions. They're rare, exceptional, divine acts that have nothing to do with human prayers, gifts, or ministries. According to that line of thinking, when someone gets healed today, it wasn't through the gift of healings but through God's providence. The gifts of the Spirit are ceased.

But here's the tension: If God still heals (and we agree He does), why would He no longer choose to do so through human obedience, faith, and compassion like He did throughout the Gospels and the early Church? When Jesus healed, He often touched people. He spoke words, listened to pain, and invited faith. He didn't *have* to do any of that, but He chose to. Why? Because He was revealing the nature of the Father through human contact. He speaks now through you. He listens now through you.

After the Resurrection, Jesus commissioned His disciples to preach, cast out demons, and lay hands on the sick: "'As the Father sent me, so I send you.' Then he breathed on them and said, 'Receive the Holy

Spirit'" (John 20:21–22 GNT). Now, you may read that passage and think, *He gave that to the apostles, not us.* Well, He also told them to go into all the world, and you don't believe that ceased, do you?

Tune in here. Get over the barriers to superbloom. There is so much more available for us by the Spirit and all He has deposited in us. Be careful limiting God and hiding behind a doctrine. What if you're the one He wrote this book for?

When the Spirit came at Pentecost, there wasn't just a symbolic flame. There was power. Tangible, transferable, mission-driven power. Paul said the Spirit gives gifts, "distributing to each one individually as He wills" (1 Corinthians 12:11 NKJV) for the common good. Among those gifts are healings and miracles. Nowhere does Scripture say those gifts were temporary. Nowhere does it say that once we had the Bible, we wouldn't need power anymore. If anything, Scripture says we'd need *more* power as the darkness grows.

Yes, God can heal without our help. He can also preach in dreams and do a lot of other stuff without our help. But He chose to work through us. That's why James writes, "Is anyone among you sick? Let them call the elders of the church to pray over them and anoint them with oil in the name of the Lord" (James 5:14).

The gifts reveal that the kingdom is here. That the name still saves. And they invite you and me to participate, not as experts or elites but as willing sons and daughters carrying the touch of heaven everywhere we go.

WALKING IN POWER WHILE YOU WAIT

Some of the most powerful miracle carriers I know are still waiting for their own.

- Joel prays for healing while needing healing.

- Nick prays for new limbs while living without them.

This is the mystery: God entrusts His power to those who will never use it for their own glory.

You don't need to be whole to carry healing. You don't need to be fixed to work miracles. You just need to be close to the name. The greatest healing isn't in your body but in your soul.

The greatest miracle isn't walking out of a hospital. It's walking into relationship with *Yeshua*, the Lord who saves you. And when He moves through you and the gifts flow through your life, it's not to make you look great. It's to lift up His name, the name above all names: Jesus.

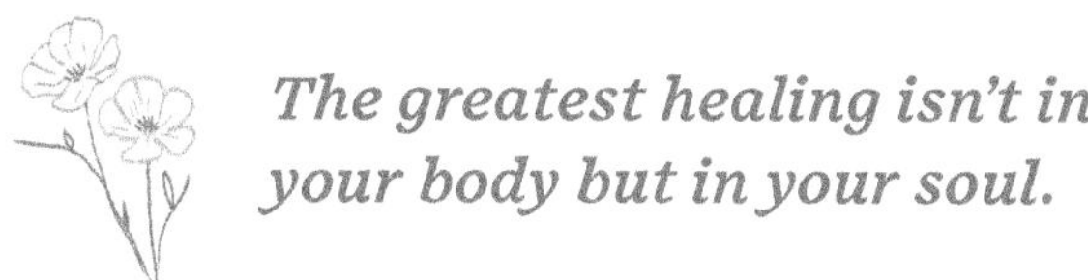

The greatest healing isn't in your body but in your soul.

BE THE MIRACLE: HEALING FROM THE INSIDE OUT

I want to close this chapter with something that's both simple and incredibly personal. When John wrote to Gaius, he said, "Dear friend, I pray that you may enjoy good health and that all may go well with you, even as your soul is getting along well" (3 John 2). That one sentence carries a vision for healing that's far bigger than we usually talk about.

It's not just physical. It's holistic. It's healing from the inside out.

That's what it means to be *pneumatikos*, a spiritual person. Not just gifted or powerful or passionate. But healed. Whole. Someone who walks with the Spirit in such a way that the life of God flows from the deepest part of you into the world around you.

That's what the Church needs right now.

A people who carry the miracle.

A people who are the miracle.

Healing from Anxiety and Emotional Wounds

There's a silent epidemic of anxiety, depression, and emotional fatigue running through the Church right now. We're ministering to others while limping inside. We're parenting from an empty tank. We're believing for healing for others while quietly battling darkness in our own minds.

Anxiety is more than stress. It's a signal that something inside you is crying out for rest, for peace, and for safety. That's not weakness. That's an invitation.

But hear me clearly: You cannot walk in the gift of healings if you refuse to let God heal your anxious heart. You cannot carry miracles to others if you're still trapped in cycles of fear, comparison, and self-hatred. I say this with compassion, not condemnation. Jesus wants to meet you there. He wants to come into the storm of your soul and speak peace, just like He did on the sea that night with His disciples. But you've got to invite Him in. You've got to come out of the darkness, out of the isolation, secrecy, numbness, and control, and into the light.

This is not hype. This is healing. And it *is* available. Some of the most powerful miracle workers I've ever known are the ones who faced their own inner battles head-on. They let God into the anxiety, trauma, and fear, and they didn't walk out the same.

Healing from Sin, Shame, and the Patterns We Chose

We already unpacked this in Chapter 5, but it bears repeating here: Many people are blocked from healing others because they haven't allowed God to heal what they've buried. The things they've done. The patterns they've fed. The wounds they've numbed.

Some of the most codependent and toxic people are the caretakers of everyone else; they "fix" their own pain with the high of being needed. Ask me how I know. I've been there.

Sin needs more than forgiveness. It needs healing. When James wrote, "Confess your sins to each other and pray for each other so that you may be healed" (James 5:16), he wasn't being poetic. He was being prophetic. There is healing power when the light comes in.

Many believers are trapped because they're still hiding, still blaming, or still carrying shame they were never meant to hold. Healing doesn't mean pretending your past didn't happen. It means allowing Jesus to come into it, breathe on it, re-narrate it, and break the cycle so it doesn't define you anymore.

We know God forgives sins, but it's time we realized He heals sinners. He restores purity. He restores courage. He restores the parts of us that addiction and pride tried to destroy. And then He gives those healed hands a gift: the power to heal others.

Healing the Physical Body

Let's talk about physical healing, because it matters. Jesus healed people everywhere He went. And He never stopped. He still heals today.

The gift of healings and the working of miracles aren't about theatrics. They are about compassion. They are a tangible expression of the Father's love through the Spirit's power. But they also require something very few people talk about: a faith that is deeply relational.

The people I know who walk in healing, people like Joel, Larry, and Nick, don't treat healing like magic. They walk in it like friendship.

They know the Healer.

They trust Him.

They submit to Him daily.

And when they speak, it's not empty hype or desperate pleading; it's agreement with heaven.

Their mouths are full of expectation, love, and worship, not entitlement. Their declarations are rooted in trust and dependence, not performance. Their prayers carry weight because they come from a life that has been refined in the fire.

- I've heard Joel pray for people's healing just hours after being hooked to dialysis.

- I've seen Nick lay hands on the sick with no arms or hands.

- I've seen Larry worship through his pain while the presence of God filled the room with glory.

None of them demands or throws up empty hype. All of them know the Healer.

That's what it looks like to walk by faith. It's not arrogance. It's not pretending. It's a quiet, unshakable confidence in the One who still heals. That kind of faith doesn't have to shout. It just knows.

There's a reason I'm ending this chapter this way. I believe that God wants to heal you and that He wants to heal through you. He wants you to carry His touch into your family, your workplace, your church, and your city. The only way it starts is with surrender.

The superbloom begins away from the spotlight, deep in the soil. It begins when the Spirit rains on the dry, hidden places of your life, and something begins to stir. Before you know it, what was dormant starts to bloom. And when it does, people around you get healed.

Don't wait for the perfect moment. Don't wait to feel powerful. Lay hands on the sick. Speak words of healing. Invite the Spirit to work through you. And if you need healing? Ask. Receive. Open your heart.

This is what Jesus does. He makes the desert bloom. And He's not done. Not with you.

Not with the Church. Not with the world He came to save.

Be the miracle. Believe again.

CHAPTER 9 STUDY GUIDE

Dear friend, I pray that you may enjoy good health and that all may go well with you, even as your soul is getting along well.

—3 John 2

REVIEW

The gifts of healings and the working of miracles reveal God's compassionate heart through supernatural power that restores bodies, suspends natural law, and demonstrates His authority. Yet these impact gifts also expose deep theological tensions. Why does one family experience healing while another buries a child?

As we explore powerful testimonies in the body of Christ, we discover that faith is not a formula but a relationship with the Healer. The Old Testament covenant names of God, such as *Jehovah Rapha* (The Lord Who Heals), reveal that healing flows from His nature, not our performance. And when we recognize that Jesus Himself is the point, not the miracle, we can overcome the four common struggles related to healing: misunderstanding God's will, misplacing the purpose of faith, carrying wounds from unanswered prayers, and defaulting to extremes.

These gifts of healings and the working of miracles are still available today because God's compassion hasn't diminished and His Spirit hasn't changed. He works through ordinary people with surrendered hearts who know the Healer. The superbloom of these gifts begins from the inside out, as the Spirit rains on dry ground and produces whole people who carry God's touch everywhere they go.

KEY SCRIPTURES

Is anyone among you sick? Let them call the elders of the church to pray over them and anoint them with oil in the name of the Lord. (James 5:14)

Jesus said to her, "I am the resurrection and the life. The one who believes in me will live, even though they die." (John 11:25)

My grace is sufficient for you, for my power is made perfect in weakness. (2 Corinthians 12:9)

Then will the eyes of the blind be opened,
    and the ears of the deaf unstopped.
Then will the lame leap like a deer,
    and the mute tongue shout for joy. (Isaiah 35:5–6)

GROUP DISCUSSION

1. How can we hold space for testimonies of dramatic healing *and* stories of faithful suffering without invalidating either experience? What language or responses help versus hurt when someone shares their pain about unanswered prayers for healing?

2. Which of the four struggles with healing ministry do you see most commonly creating damage in church settings? How can we address these misunderstandings while still pursuing the genuine gifts?

3. How does the Lazarus story reframe the purpose of miracles and shift our focus from outcomes to relationship?

4. How does understanding God's covenant names as revelations of His nature (rather than conditional promises) change our expectations about healing? How does Jesus embody all these names?

5. How do Joel's and Nick's testimonies challenge our assumptions about who God uses in healing ministry? What does this reveal about God's trust and the purpose of these gifts?

PERSONAL REFLECTION

1. What barriers prevent you from positioning yourself to be used in the impact gifts? How can you take one step of faith forward this week?

2. What would change in your prayer life if you truly believed Jesus Himself is enough, even when the tomb stays sealed?

3. What hidden, unhealed places might be blocking your ability to carry God's touch to others? What would it look like to invite Jesus into those places?

4. In what situations might God be calling you to be the miracle through practical acts of compassion, provision, and presence rather than waiting for supernatural intervention?

PRAYER

Father God, thank You for the greatest miracle of Your presence in our lives. Open our eyes and hearts to what Your Spirit wants to do in and through us. Fill us with the courage to pray bold prayers of faith. When theological dissonance tempts us to doubt, remind us that You are enough. When we don't understand Your timing, help us remember that Your goodness rests in Your nature, not our circumstances. Heal us from the inside out so we can carry Your touch to others. May our lives reveal the Healer who still restores today. In Jesus' name, Amen.

10

THE FAITHFUL STEWARD

Living the Superbloom

By journeying honestly, I hope we can go beyond our current
understanding of the Holy Spirit and begin to commune openly … that
our experience with Him would be day by day, even moment by moment.
That by keeping in step with the Spirit, we might regularly fellowship over
what He's doing rather than what He did months or years ago.

—**Francis Chan**, *Forgotten God*

Since we live by the Spirit, let us keep in step with the Spirit.

—**Galatians 5:25**

THE EMAIL CAME at 6:47 on a Tuesday morning.

> Pastor Jeff, I need to tell you what happened yesterday. After read-
> ing your book and going through the training, I finally understood
> what you meant about being Spirit-activated instead of just Spirit-
> filled. I was at my daughter's school pickup, and the Lord gave me a
> word for another mom I barely know. I was terrified, but I stepped
> out in faith. Turns out, it was exactly what she needed to hear in
> the middle of a marriage crisis. She started crying right there in
> the carpool line and asked if I could pray with her. Pastor, I've been
> a Christian for twenty years, but I've never experienced anything
> like this. How do I live like this every day?

That email represents thousands of conversations I've had over the
past few years. These people have moved beyond just understanding

spiritual gifts to actually walking in them. They've discovered the difference between being filled with the Spirit and being activated by the Spirit. They are the ones living the superbloom.

I've learned there's a massive gap between having a powerful spiritual experience and developing a *sustainable* Spirit-activated lifestyle. It's one thing to prophesy at a conference. It's another to hear God's voice while you're changing diapers. Witnessing a healing during a prayer meeting is powerful, but do you carry that anointing into your workplace on Monday morning? You feel the incredible power of God during worship, yet being sensitive to the Spirit while you're stuck in traffic or dealing with difficult family members tests if that power has truly transformed you.

Supernatural experiences are one thing. A supernatural life is something so much more.

THE INTEGRATION CHALLENGE

I wish someone had told me twenty years ago that spiritual gifts without spiritual integration create chaos. I've seen people who can't maintain healthy relationships receive powerful prophetic words. I've watched believers who can't manage their own emotional wounds move in healing. I've known folks who operate in discernment during church services but make terrible personal decisions the rest of the week.

The gifts are real. The power is available. But if you don't learn how to integrate what you've received into the fabric of daily life, you'll end up like the Corinthians who were gifted but immature, powerful but problematic.

Paul puts it this way: "When I was a child, I talked like a child, I thought like a child, I reasoned like a child. When I became a man, I put the ways of childhood behind me" (1 Corinthians 13:11). Gifts are not graduation; they're kindergarten.

Can you move in spiritual gifts? If you're a believer, then the answer is yes. But can you also steward them with the wisdom and maturity that honors God and serves others? That's what this chapter is about: getting and *staying* activated. You can experience the superbloom *and* live it sustainably for decades to come.

THE FIVE-PART ACTIVATION PROCESS

Over the past several years at Anchor Church, we've developed what we call the "Spirit-Activated Lifestyle" framework. It's built around five interconnected practices that help believers move from sporadic spiritual experiences to consistent supernatural living.

These aren't five steps you complete once and move on from. They're five ongoing rhythms that create the conditions for sustained activation. Think of them like the elements that create the perfect environment for continuous superbloom.

1. Daily Soil Preparation (Chapters 1–2 Application)

Remember what we learned in the first two chapters? The condition of your spiritual soil determines what can grow in your life. Seeds can't bloom in contaminated ground, and gifts can't flourish in unprepared hearts.

Daily soil preparation means creating consistent rhythms that keep your heart receptive to the Spirit's work. Here's what this looks like in my life:

Morning Heart Alignment

I start every day with a simple process that sets the trajectory for everything that follows. This all usually happens in the first fifteen minutes of a walk.

First, I always say, "I love You, Lord." Then, within just a few moments of being up, I will usually start to pray in the Spirit. This has become a default way of entering His presence and being with Him. It immediately tells my entire being that I am spirit, I have a soul, and I live in a body. Praying in the Spirit overwhelms any words I could come up with on my own. It's an acknowledgment in the Spirit that I know whose I am: "Lord, I'm Yours. This is all Yours. My day is Yours. My gifts are Yours. I'm here, and You are here with me."

Second, once I get into a place of thinking and processing with the Lord, I listen to His voice and engage in confessing what needs confessing: "Show me anything that would hinder Your flow through me today." This is Psalm 51 and Psalm 139 in action. He searches me and reveals me to me. I've learned that unrepentant sin, unforgiveness, and unhealed wounds create static in my spiritual signal.

Third, I read Scripture and keep thinking of Him and listening to Him. I stay submitted: "I release my agenda to Your agenda. I release my timing to Your timing. I release my methods to Your methods." I may not say those exact words, but that is my heart posture.

Finally, throughout the morning and the day I continually invite fresh filling: "Holy Spirit, fill me with Your power. Your words. Your will.

Your presence. Your agenda. Your heart. Your vision. Your gifts." This is my posture as often as I remember.

This isn't a magic formula. It's a daily alignment that keeps my heart in the condition where the Spirit can work freely.

Evening Heart Evaluation

At the end of each day, I always lift my hands and pray in the Spirit again. I reflect on everything that happened that day, declaring out loud all the times the Lord spared me, led me, empowered me, and kept me. If I sense that anything was astray, I confess it immediately. It's not a science; it's a relationship.

Before I rest, I walk through these simple steps:

- I declare out loud my only hope in Jesus.

- I praise Him for His presence, power, love, and leadership in my day.

- I give Him glory for all of the ways He allowed me to operate in His gifts through the day.

- I pray over my marriage, children, and home.

- I ask God for dreams, visions, and protection in my sleep.

The Spirit is constantly speaking, constantly moving, and constantly creating opportunities for His gifts to flow through us. The more aware we become of His rhythms, the more naturally we learn to flow with them.

Regular Soil Assessment

Once or twice a month, usually an hour before my time with my coach and therapist, I do a deeper evaluation of my spiritual soil. I use a simple framework based on what we learned in Chapters 1–2:

- **Sincere Faith**: I work at the deepest motive levels by engaging in the parts of my heart. This work is layered in paying attention to emotions and the patterns of my thinking and habits.

- **Clear Conscience**: I have practiced mastering Psalm 51. I bring the Lord into the categories of my heart and have Him reveal any secret sin(s) I can't see. I pay attention to the depths of my words, patterns, attitudes, fears, ambitions, and more. He cleans me in this, and I confess it in detail to my therapist and his wife.

- **Surrendered Will**: I submit the entire framework of the church, ministry, and strategy, as well as all my concerns and fears.

- **Healed Heart**: If there are any offenses that come up from the people closest to me, I get perspective on those hurts with the Lord and receive healing.

This regular assessment helps me identify what might be hindering the flow of spiritual gifts through my life and take corrective action before small issues become major blockages.

At Anchor Church, we've created several daily prayer journals and online resources to help people develop these rhythms. Visit myanchorchurch.com/resources to learn more. But remember: Tools aren't magic. They're just helps. The key is consistency in preparing your heart for what God wants to do through you.

2. Gift Recognition and Activation (Chapter 3 Application)

One of the biggest breakthroughs in my understanding came when I realized the difference between having gifts and activating gifts. I used to think that everyone gets a gift, kind of like how every kid gets a present at Christmas.

I no longer see it this way. Why? Because I've studied the text and because I continually operate in all of the gifts as the Spirit wills. He speaks through me, heals through me, works miracles through me, gives words of knowledge and wisdom through me, discerns spirits through me, and manifests powerful surges of faith through me.

Now, there are some gifts where I see different levels of impact and fruit, but that's according to God's will through me and the anointing He has given me. This is much more about learning how to know Him and recognize His presence than "having a gift." Otherwise, it would be like having a smartphone but only using it to make phone calls. The capacities for texting, internet, photography, and countless applications are built into the device, but if you don't know how to activate those features, you'll never benefit from them.

Identifying Your Gift Mix

While every believer has access to all the gifts as the Spirit wills, most people have what I call a "gift mix" of two or three gifts that flow most naturally through their personality, calling, and life circumstances.

For me, I tend to operate in the gifts of faith, prophecy, words of knowledge, words of wisdom, and tongues more than the other gifts. I do not regularly operate in healings. I used to when I did more counseling and intervention type ministry. I'm able to minister in all of the gifts, but some are more normative in my life.

Some people naturally lean toward the revelation gifts (prophecy, discernment, words of knowledge). Others flow more easily in the power gifts (faith, healings, miracles). Still others find the communication gifts (tongues, interpretations) come most readily.

Understanding your gift mix isn't about limiting what God can do through you. He can do anything He wants. Understanding your gift mix is about recognizing the primary channels through which He tends to work in your life so you can steward them well and create opportunities for growth in other areas.

How to identify and activate your gift mix:

START WITH SCRIPTURE MEDITATION

> Each of you should use whatever gift you have received to serve others, as faithful stewards of God's grace in its various forms. If anyone speaks, they should do so as one who speaks the very words of God. If anyone serves, they should do so with the strength God provides, so that in all things God may be praised through Jesus Christ. To him be the glory and the power for ever and ever. Amen. (1 Peter 4:10–11)

I recommend spending focused time meditating on 1 Peter 4 and other gift passages, such as 1 Corinthians 12, Romans 12, and Ephesians 4. Ask the Holy Spirit to highlight which gifts resonate most deeply with your heart. Often, the gifts you find yourself most drawn to are the ones God wants to develop first in your life.

PRACTICE IN SAFE ENVIRONMENTS

At Anchor, we create multiple environments where people can practice developing their gifts without pressure or performance anxiety. Our Healing Ministry training groups, Prophetic Ministry classes, and Prayer Ministry teams provide safe spaces to step out in faith, make mistakes, and learn from experienced practitioners.

You don't have to wait for a formal training program, though. You can start practicing on your own, with trusted friends, or in small group settings where people understand you're learning.

KEEP A GIFT JOURNAL

I'm not the best at this, but when I do it, it's so powerful. I encourage people to keep track of how they sense the Spirit moving through them. When do you get supernatural insights about people? When do you feel unusual faith for healing? When do you find yourself praying in tongues more freely? When do you sense God giving you words of encouragement that seem to go beyond your natural wisdom?

Some people keep a journal for gifts, ministries, and testimonies. Remember Sky, back in Chapter 8? The reason I had access to that prophecy and word of knowledge is because I journaled it during the time of my son's tragedy. Having access to the ministry of the Holy Spirit during that time built my faith so much over the days ahead.

I'm thankful for all the ways I'm able to look back and see the hand of God. He uses testimony, remembering, and journaling to deepen the richness of the soil of your heart and ministry.

The most significant shift in this book is a crucial mindset adjustment. Instead of praying, "God, give me the gift of prophecy," start praying, "God, activate the prophetic deposit You've already placed in me." Instead of asking for more of the Spirit, start asking the Spirit to have more of you. This is *everything*. The gifts are already there. Your job isn't to acquire them but to access them.

3. Spirit Sensitivity Development (Chapters 4–6 Application)

Multiple people have asked me, "How do you just flow? How do you operate in the gifts all the time, it seems?" I always say, "Walking in the Spirit is the flow of the Christian life." This is why praying in the Spirit is such a powerful blessing. It keeps you in His Spirit and out of your flesh. As a matter of fact, nothing moves me out of the flesh into the Spirit as fast as praying in the Spirit.

Learning to live under the influence of the Holy Spirit requires spiritual sensitivity, which is the ability to discern the difference between what's from God, what's from your own soul, and what's from the enemy. This is where many people get stuck. They have genuine spiritual experiences, but they lack the discernment to steward them wisely. They end up either dismissing everything as imagination or accepting everything as divine, both of which lead to problems.

Several times throughout each day, I do what I now call an "influence check." Too much coffee, too much X, too much politics, too much comparison, and too much planning contaminate my soul. I can feel it.

So I pause and ask myself, *What's influencing me right now? Am I operating under the influence of the Spirit, or am I being driven by my flesh, lust, pride, fear, slothfulness, greed, gluttony, anger, or what?*

- Peace Check: What is disturbing the peace of Christ in my heart?

- Fruit Check: What is affecting the fruit of the Spirit (love, joy, peace, etc.) in me?

- Word Check: What messages are going unfiltered through me? Why?

This is about awareness, not perfection. The more conscious you become of what's driving your thoughts, emotions, and decisions, the more you can align yourself with the Spirit's leading.

Developing Spiritual Disciplines for Discernment

Just like a radio needs to be tuned to the right frequency to receive clear signals, your spirit needs to be tuned to the Holy Spirit's frequency to receive clear guidance.

I've found that certain practices significantly increase my spiritual sensitivity:

- **Extended Time in God's Presence**: I have regular periods of worship, prayer, and simply being still before God, tuning my heart to His voice and His ways.

- **Scripture Saturation**: I fill myself with the Bible throughout the day. The more familiar I am with God's written Word, the more easily I recognize His voice in other forms. The Spirit never contradicts Scripture; He always illuminates it.

- **Fasting and Simplicity**: I fast every week, three days every month, and twenty-one days twice a year. Nothing resets my whole life like denying my physical appetites. When my flesh is quiet, my spirit can hear more clearly, and I am more sensitive to spiritual realities.

- **Community Confirmation**: I am very transparent with my therapists, my wife, my elders, my senior team, and my closest friends. I do not have secrets in my life. Everything in me is open, at least at the therapist level and in appropriate ways with those closest to me. I have many people in my life who are close enough to help confirm what I sense the Spirit doing. They all have permission to speak clearly about what they see too.

- **Learning to Wait**: I'm infinitely more patient today than I've ever been. Sometimes the most spiritual thing you can do is wait. If you're not sure whether something is from God, wait until you have clarity. God is patient, and His guidance becomes clearer over time.

4. Gift Development and Flow (Chapters 7–9 Application)

Once you're regularly recognizing and stewarding the gifts God has placed in your life, the next level is learning how they work together and how to develop greater proficiency in each area.

Understanding Gift Progression

In my experience, the gifts tend to develop in a natural progression:

Faith → Discernment → Tongues → Prophecy → Healings

- Faith is the foundation. You learn to trust God for things beyond your natural ability.

- Discernment builds on that foundation. You learn to distinguish between different spiritual influences.

- Tongues often opens the door to other gifts. You receive a personal prayer language that connects you to the Spirit's flow.

- Prophetic words flow from that connection. You speak God's heart to others.

- Healings and Miracles often emerge as you become more confident in the other gifts, extending God's power to bring restoration.

This doesn't mean that you have to master one gift before moving to the next or that they always develop in this order. But I've noticed this pattern in my own life and in hundreds of people I've helped train in gift development.

Creating Flow Opportunities

The gifts of the Spirit are like muscles: They need to be exercised regularly to stay strong and develop properly. This means you need to create opportunities to use them, even when it feels uncomfortable or risky.

You may notice if you're ever in a 21 Days of Prayer atmosphere, almost everyone who participates ends up operating in multiple gifts of the Spirit. It's not because they "have a gift." It's because they're cultivating the soil and activating without distraction throughout that time.

The anointing for ministry always increases with obedient practice. At Anchor, we build gift development into our regular church life:

- During small group prayer times, we encourage people to step out with prophecy, words of knowledge, or healing prayer.

- Our Sunday services include space for testimony, prophecy, and prayer for healing. It happens throughout the room every week (not necessarily from the platform but all throughout the house).

- We have regular training intensives where people can practice in safe, instructed environments.

- We have teams on mission initiatives and trips where people can step out in faith in evangelistic contexts. This always increases gift and ministry activation.

The key is moving from being a consumer of spiritual gifts to being a practitioner. Again, you don't have to wait for formal church programs. You can start creating flow opportunities in your own life today:

- Pray for people's healing when they mention physical problems to you.

- Ask God for words of encouragement for people in your daily interactions.

- Practice praying in tongues during your personal prayer time.

- Step out with supernatural faith for breakthrough in your own circumstances.

Handling Mistakes Gracefully

Here's something nobody talks about enough: You're going to make mistakes as you learn to operate in spiritual gifts. You'll give prophecies that don't quite hit the mark. You'll pray for healing and see no immediate change. You'll step out in faith and feel like you missed God's leading.

That's not failure. It's simply part of the learning process. Every person I know who moves powerfully in the gifts went through a season of awkward attempts, partial successes, and outright misses. The difference between those who develop proficiency and those who give up is how they handle the mistakes.

- **Learn from your misses.** When something doesn't go as expected, ask God what you can learn from the experience. Were you operating in presumption rather than faith? Were you trying to perform rather than simply obeying? Were you motivated by your ego rather than God's love?

- **Always get back up.** Don't let one bad experience shut you down. The enemy's goal is to use your mistakes to convince you that you're not called to move in spiritual gifts. God's goal is to use your mistakes to develop humility, wisdom, and greater sensitivity to His voice.

- **Find the right mentors.** Connect with people who move in the gifts with maturity and ask them to help you process your experiences. Most people who operate powerfully in spiritual gifts are eager to help others develop.

5. Kingdom Multiplication
(Chapter 1 Application)

The final element of living a Spirit-activated lifestyle is learning to be a catalyst for others' activation. Don't be a solo consumer of your own spiritual experiences. The goal of your personal superbloom goes beyond your own fulfillment into developing conditions for corporate and kingdom-level transformation. You're meant to be a planter of other people's spiritual seeds, not just a tender of your own garden.

Becoming a Gift Developer

Once you've developed some proficiency in recognizing and stewarding spiritual gifts in your own life, God will start bringing people across your path who need help discovering what He's placed in them. You don't have to be a professional minister or spiritual teacher to help others access what God has already given them. Here's what this looks like practically:

- **Create safe spaces.** You needed safe environments to practice developing your gifts, and others need the same thing. Host small groups in your home where people can pray for each other, practice prophecy, or step out in faith for healing.

- **Share your story.** Be open about your own journey of discovering and developing spiritual gifts. Your testimony will give others permission to pursue what God has for them.

- **Pray activation prayers.** When you're praying with people, ask God to activate what He's placed in them, not just to meet their immediate needs. Pray for their gift development, their spiritual sensitivity, and their boldness to step out in faith.

- **Encourage risk-taking.** Many people know they're called to move in spiritual gifts but are paralyzed by the fear of making mistakes. Be the voice that encourages them to step out, try, learn, and grow.

Planting Seeds for the Future

The most exciting aspect of living a Spirit-activated lifestyle is recognizing that what God does through you has the potential to impact generations beyond your own lifetime. Every person you help activate their spiritual gifts becomes a catalyst for activating others. Every healing you pray for creates faith in someone else to step out for breakthrough. Every prophetic word you give encourages someone else to listen for God's voice.

Yes, you're pursuing a personal spiritual experience, but you're also participating in a movement of the Spirit that's intended to transform the Church and impact the world. This generational perspective changes how you approach gift development. Beyond having powerful spiritual experiences yourself, you can become the kind of person who helps facilitate powerful spiritual experiences for others.

SEASONS OF SPIRITUAL DROUGHT

Even people who live Spirit-activated lifestyles go through seasons where the gifts seem less active, the voice of God seems quieter, and spiritual breakthrough seems more difficult.

This isn't a sign that you've lost what God gave you or that you're somehow failing spiritually. Sometimes, it's actually evidence that God is taking you deeper.

Understanding Spiritual Seasons

Just like natural seasons, spiritual seasons serve different purposes.

- **Spring** awakens new growth, fresh vision, and emerging gift development. Everything feels exciting and full of potential.

- **Summer** releases fruitfulness, active ministry, and powerful spiritual experiences. This is when the gifts flow most easily.

- **Fall** delivers harvest and consolidation. You see the fruit of previous growth and help others develop what God has given them.

- **Winter** provides rest, reflection, and deeper root development. The gifts may seem less active, but God is doing important work beneath the surface.

Each season is necessary. Trying to stay in perpetual summer leads to burnout, while trying to avoid winter leads to shallow development.

Navigating Drought with Faith

Here is a guide for any season when spiritual gifts seem less active:

- **Don't panic.** God hasn't abandoned you or taken back what He's given you. He may be preparing you for a new level of development.

- **Stay faithful.** Continue your daily rhythms of prayer, Scripture reading, and worship, even when you don't feel particularly spiritual. Faithfulness in the dry seasons prepares you for fruitfulness in the growing seasons.

- **Seek wise counsel.** Connect with mature believers who can help you discern what God might be doing in this season. Sometimes an outside perspective can see what we miss.

- **Focus on character.** Use seasons of spiritual drought to focus on character development, relational health, and growth in areas of your life that need attention. God often uses these seasons to address foundational issues that need to be strengthened.

- **Trust the process.** Remember that gift development is a lifelong journey, not a one-time event. God is more committed to your spiritual growth than you are, and He knows exactly what you need in every season.

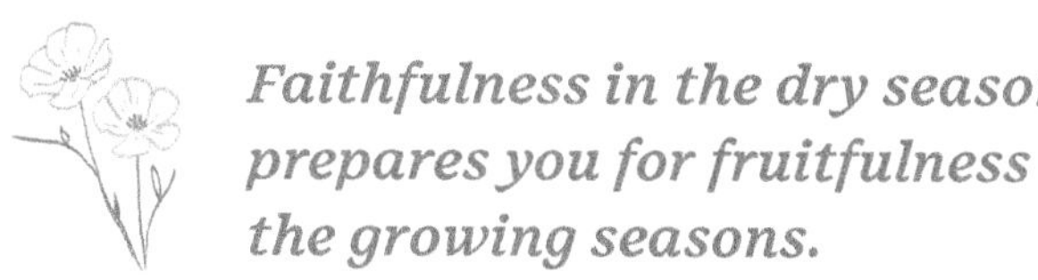

Faithfulness in the dry seasons prepares you for fruitfulness in the growing seasons.

BUILDING COMMUNITY THAT SUPPORTS SUPERBLOOM

One of the most important aspects of living a Spirit-activated lifestyle is surrounding yourself with people who share your commitment to spiritual growth and gift development. This doesn't mean isolating yourself from non-believers or less spiritually mature Christians. But it does mean intentionally building relationships with people who will encourage your spiritual development rather than discourage it.

Look for people who

- share your hunger for more of God's presence and power.

- are willing to take risks in stepping out in spiritual gifts.

- provide both encouragement and accountability.

- have experience in areas where you're still learning.

- are committed to long-term spiritual growth rather than just dramatic experiences.

These relationships might develop through church small groups, ministry teams, training classes, or informal friendships. The key is finding people who understand that spiritual gifts are meant to be developed and exercised, not just talked about.

Creating Activation Culture

If you can't find a community that supports gift development, consider creating one. Start a small group in your home focused on practicing spiritual gifts. Organize prayer meetings where people can step out in prophecy and healing. Host dinners where conversation naturally turns to what God is doing in people's lives.

At Anchor Church, we've learned that activation culture doesn't happen accidentally; it has to be intentionally cultivated. We're nowhere near where we want to be, but it is so refreshing to see the superbloom start. It's Him!

We've seen that once the mindset of freedom takes root, it is sustained as people begin to experience the joy of moving in spiritual gifts and helping others learn to as well.

Dealing with Opposition and Misunderstanding

Living a Spirit-activated lifestyle will inevitably bring opposition and misunderstanding, sometimes from unexpected sources. Family members may think you've become fanatical. Church friends may accuse you of going overboard. Even other believers may question whether spiritual gifts are still active today.

This opposition isn't necessarily a sign that you're doing something wrong. Often, it's evidence that you're doing something right. The enemy doesn't waste time fighting things that don't threaten his kingdom.

When you encounter resistance to your pursuit of spiritual gifts, remember that your response can either create space for God to work or build walls that make it harder for others to hear.

- **Don't become defensive.** Defensiveness usually escalates conflict rather than resolving it. Listen to people's concerns, acknowledge their fears, and respond with patience and love.

- **Let your life speak.** The best response to theological arguments against spiritual gifts is a life that demonstrates their value. Show people the fruit of Spirit-activated living through your character, relationships, and ministry effectiveness.

- **Stay humble.** Remember that you're still learning and growing. Be quick to acknowledge mistakes and slow to claim spiritual superiority over others.

- **Build bridges, not barriers.** Look for common ground with people who have different perspectives on spiritual gifts. Focus on shared commitments to loving God, serving others, and advancing His kingdom.

- **Keep learning.** Study Scripture carefully so you can give thoughtful responses to theological questions. Read books by respected scholars who support the continuation of spiritual gifts. Seek mentorship from mature believers who can help you navigate controversial issues wisely.

YOUR SUPERBLOOM STARTS NOW

As we conclude this exploration of how to live a Spirit-activated lifestyle, I want to leave you with both a challenge and an encouragement.

Challenge

God has deposited supernatural power in your life and given you access to the same Spirit that raised Jesus from the dead. He's equipped you with gifts that can bring healing to the broken, hope to the discouraged, and life to the dead.

But everything you've learned in this book is worthless unless you actually apply it. It's like reading about swimming: You can understand the theory perfectly, but you'll never actually swim until you get in the water. Spiritual gifts will remain dormant unless you activate them through faith, develop them through practice, and steward them through maturity.

Encouragement

You don't have to figure this out all at once. Spiritual development is a marathon, not a sprint. God is more patient with your growth than you are, and He's more committed to your success than you could ever be.

So start where you are. Use what you have. Do what you can. If you've never prayed for someone's healing, step out in faith. If you've never asked God for a prophetic word for someone, try that. If you've never prayed in tongues, ask the Holy Spirit to give you that gift.

Don't wait until you feel ready or perfectly prepared or fully confident that all your questions are answered. The seeds are already in the ground. The rain is already falling. The only question is whether you'll step into the superbloom that God has prepared for your life.

Your Personal Activation Prayer

Father, thank You for what You've deposited in my life through Your Holy Spirit. I confess that I've often lived below my spiritual potential, either through ignorance, fear, or unbelief. Today I choose to step into everything You've made available to me. I believe that I have received the total gift package with every spiritual gift, supernatural ability, and divine empowerment that I need to live a life that brings You glory and advances Your kingdom.

Activate what You've placed in me. Stir up the gifts that have been dormant. Give me supernatural sensitivity to Your voice, Your leading, and Your power. Help me to steward these gifts with wisdom, humility, and love. Use me to bring healing to the broken, hope to the discouraged, and life to the dead. Make me a catalyst for others' spiritual activation. Let my life create hunger for more of You in everyone I encounter.

I surrender my agenda to Your agenda, my timing to Your timing, my methods to Your methods. Have Your way in my life, Lord. Let the superbloom begin. In Jesus' name, Amen.

THE VISION FOR WHAT WE COULD BECOME

I want to leave you with the vision that drives everything we do at Anchor Church and everything I've written in this book. I believe God is preparing to pour out His Spirit in a way that will awaken gifts that have been lying dormant for generations. I believe we're about to see ordinary believers discover extraordinary power. I believe the Church is about to bloom in ways that will astonish the world.

But it starts with individuals like you who are willing to believe that God still speaks, still heals, still moves in power, and still wants to work through ordinary people who make themselves available. Just imagine what would happen if every believer in your church discovered and developed the spiritual gifts God has placed in them. Picture the impact your community would experience if healings, prophecy, miracles, and divine wisdom became normal parts of church life. Envision what would happen if your workplace, your neighborhood, your family experienced the presence and power of God through your Spirit-activated life.

That's not fantasy or hype or a far-off "someday." It's potential. It's hope. And it's today, if you'll step into what God has already made available to you. The seeds are in the soil. The rain is falling. The time is here.

Your superbloom starts now.

CHAPTER 10 STUDY GUIDE

When I was a child, I talked like a child, I thought like a child, I reasoned like a child. When I became a man, I put the ways of childhood behind me.

—1 Corinthians 13:11

REVIEW

Living the superbloom means moving beyond sporadic spiritual experiences to a sustainable Spirit-activated lifestyle. It's about learning to carry the supernatural into ordinary life. Yes, the gifts are real, and the power is available. But when spiritual gifts aren't integrated into character and maturity, they create chaos instead of fruitfulness. The goal goes beyond having singular powerful moments and extends to developing consistent supernatural living that honors God and serves others.

The five-part activation framework provides ongoing rhythms for sustained growth: daily soil preparation (alignment and evaluation), gift recognition and activation (shifting from "I need more" to "I need activation"), Spirit sensitivity development (learning to discern God's voice from other influences), gift development and flow (creating opportunities to practice and handling mistakes gracefully), and kingdom multiplication (becoming a catalyst for others' activation).

Understanding gift progression helps believers steward what flows naturally while remaining open to how God may move in any moment. Every spiritual season serves a purpose, and even droughts help to develop deeper roots. A supernatural life requires supportive community, gracious responses to opposition, and reminders that spiritual development is a marathon, not a sprint. The seeds are planted, the rain is falling, and your superbloom starts now.

KEY SCRIPTURES

Each of you should use whatever gift you have received to serve others, as faithful stewards of God's grace in its various forms. If anyone speaks, they should do so as one who speaks the very words of God. If anyone serves, they should do so with the strength God provides, so that in all things God may be praised through Jesus Christ. To him be the glory and the power for ever and ever. Amen. (1 Peter 4:10–11)

And if the Spirit of him who raised Jesus from the dead is living in you, he who raised Christ from the dead will also give life to your mortal bodies because of his Spirit who lives in you. (Romans 8:11)

But the fruit of the Spirit is love, joy, peace, forbearance, kindness, goodness, faithfulness, gentleness and self-control. Against such things there is no law. (Galatians 5:22–23)

Create in me a pure heart, O God,
  and renew a steadfast spirit within me.
Do not cast me from your presence
  or take your Holy Spirit from me.

Restore to me the joy of your salvation
  and grant me a willing spirit, to sustain me. (Psalm 51:10–12)

GROUP DISCUSSION

1. How does the distinction between "Spirit-filled" and "Spirit-activated" change our understanding of daily Christian living?

2. What common barriers prevent people from moving beyond powerful weekend experiences to supernatural living throughout the week? How can we break through these barriers?

3. Which of the five activation practices (daily soil preparation, gift recognition, Spirit sensitivity, gift development, kingdom multiplication) seems most natural for believers to develop? Which feels most challenging?

4. What would it look like to create an environment where people feel empowered to step out in faith, make mistakes, and learn together? What guidelines or values would help create healthy activation culture?

5. How can believers help each other navigate different spiritual seasons and opposition gracefully?

PERSONAL REFLECTION

1. Where are you today on the continuum between powerful spiritual experiences and a sustainable Spirit-activated lifestyle? Where would you like to be?

2. Which two or three gifts seem to flow most naturally through your life right now? How could you create more opportunities to practice these gifts while remaining open to other manifestations as the Spirit wills?

3. How does understanding spiritual seasons help you trust God's process in your life?

4. How are you currently helping others discover and develop their spiritual gifts? What would it look like for you to move toward "legacy thinking" in how you steward what God has given you?

PRAYER

Father God, thank You for depositing supernatural power in our lives through Your Holy Spirit. By faith, we say yes to everything You've made available to us. Activate what You've placed in us and stir up every dormant gift. Give us supernatural sensitivity to Your voice, Your leading, and Your power. Help us steward these gifts with wisdom, humility, and love. Move us from sporadic experiences to sustainable supernatural living. Let our lives create hunger for more of You in everyone we encounter. We surrender to Your perfect plan and timing. Have Your way in us. In Jesus' name, Amen.

CONCLUSION

It is not great talents God blesses so much as great likeness to Jesus.

—**Robert Murray M'Cheyne**

Now it is required that those who have been given a trust must prove faithful.

—**1 Corinthians 4:2**

THIS BOOK IS a miracle. I sat down to write it in my cabin in Montana, and the Lord graced me to finish the entire manuscript in six days. I can't tell you how many other times I have sat down to write and left with nothing but outlines and distractions.

Again, this sabbatical is so profoundly different from the last time I was here. There's a fresh anointing on the Church right now. I know it personally. We've all seen the shaking of mega-churches in America in the past few years. We've all seen the elitism of successful ministry in the name of Jesus. It's left us all wanting more.

Even as I sit here, I'm wrestling with what to do about our growth. We need a bigger facility, but *do we really*? I honestly don't know, but I'm listening. God knows what we need.

The difference right now is one word: contentment. If I could give you one thing I've learned from pouring into this book, it's that I have learned to be content with the One who lives in me and has filled me with inexpressible and glorious joy.

If He wants a facility in our city, He'll speak it. I'm content with Him.

If He wants to plant churches, He'll activate them. I'm content with Him.

If He wants to write a book through me, He'll write it. I'm content with Him.

When you get to the core of Spirit-activated, Spirit-fueled ministry, you'll experience an overwhelming peace and contentment. Every gift of the Spirit is rooted in sensing and knowing His presence, His heart, and His will in the moment. That is maturity. That is *pneumatikos*.

THE HEART OF IT ALL

My younger brother, Jason Jenkins, is now fifty years old. Besides sharing the same parents, we also shared a room for eighteen years. Our DNA and our experiences are so similar. People tell us both all the time, "Man, y'all's mannerisms are identical. It's freaky."

As I sit here, overwhelmed by gratitude for how God has worked in my life and excited about what He wants to do through the people who will read this book, I keep coming back to one simple truth: None of this is really about spiritual gifts.

It's really about relationship. It's about living your life in such a way that people who hang out with you will say, "Man, I can tell you know Jesus and carry His Spirit. Y'all's mannerisms are identical. It's freaky!"

That only happens in relationship. The gifts are more than tools; they're ways He manifests His presence through you. It's Him loving through you. The experiences are just encounters. The ministry is just opportunity. At the heart of it all is a God who loves you enough to fill you with His Spirit, trust you with His power, and invite you into partnership with His purposes.

He doesn't need you to accomplish His will in the earth. He *chooses* you.

He doesn't require your cooperation to establish His kingdom. He *invites* you.

He doesn't demand perfection before He entrusts you with spiritual gifts. He *gives* Himself to you and *works* through you as you're willing to grow.

The superbloom is about much more than what comes out of the ground of your life. It's about staying connected to the One who planted the seeds, sends the rain, controls the seasons, and will ultimately receive the glory for whatever blooms. Whether your life produces a small wildflower that encourages one person or a massive field that impacts thousands, the measure of success is the faithfulness of the steward, not the size of the bloom.

God isn't impressed by your spiritual accomplishments. He's moved by your surrendered heart. He delights in willing obedience over perfect performances. Above all, He desires a genuine relationship with you.

FAITHFUL NEXT STEPS

As you close this book and step into whatever God has prepared for your own superbloom season, remember these three foundations:

Trust what God has sown in you. Stop waiting for more and start stewarding what you already have. The gifts are there. The calling is real. The potential is enormous. You do not lack anything you need to live a Spirit-activated life.

Steward faithfully what's growing. Develop sustainable rhythms of spiritual growth. Create environments where your gifts can flourish. Surround yourself with people who encourage your development. Stay committed to the process even when progress feels slow.

Sow generously around you. Look for opportunities to plant seeds of life, hope, and supernatural possibility in every encounter. Use your gifts to serve others. Share your resources to advance God's kingdom. Live in a way that creates hunger for more of God in people around you.

Through it all, remember that the most important thing is to remain faithfully connected to the One who makes blooming possible. Because the seeds are in the ground. The rain is coming. The desert is ready to bloom.

> Now to him who is able to do immeasurably more than all we ask or imagine, according to his power that is at work within us, to him be glory in the church and in Christ Jesus throughout all generations, for ever and ever! Amen. (Ephesians 3:20–21)

Stay faithful, my friend. The harvest is coming. The superbloom is real. And you are part of it.

Best ahead,

Pastor Jeff

10 PRAYERS FOR SUPERBLOOM ACTIVATION

Therefore, my dear brothers and sisters, stand firm. Let nothing move you. Always give yourselves fully to the work of the Lord, because you know that your labor in the Lord is not in vain.

—1 Corinthians 15:58

THESE PRAYERS ARE designed to help you approach God with the pure heart and eager desire that open the door to supernatural fruitfulness. Each prayer corresponds to the theme of the corresponding chapter number and provides language for how to engage practically with what God has deposited in your life. Use them as starting points for your own conversations with the Lord, adapting them to your unique journey and circumstances.

PRAYER 1: AWAKEN WHAT'S DORMANT

PREPARING YOUR HEART

Father, I come before You acknowledging that the condition of my heart determines what can grow in my life. I confess that I've allowed contamination to settle in my spiritual soil. Unforgiveness, pride, fear, and compromise have hindered Your work in me. As David wrote in Psalm 139:23–24, "Search me, O God, and know my heart; test me and know my anxious thoughts. See if there is any offensive way in me and lead me in the way everlasting." I want to be good ground for Your Word, Your Spirit, and Your purposes. Remove the rocks of hardness, the thorns of distraction, and the shallow places of superficial commitment. Break up the fallow ground of my heart so that when You send the rain of Your Spirit, everything You've planted can bloom. I surrender my agenda, my timing, and my methods to You. Prepare me for the superbloom You've planned for my life. In Jesus' name, Amen.

PRAYER 2: SINCERE FAITH

CULTIVATING CERTAINTY IN OBEDIENCE AND REPENTANCE

Father, I want my faith to be sincere, not superficial. I confess that I've sometimes been more concerned with appearing spiritual than being genuine. I've pursued experiences more than I've pursued You. Forgive me for any mixed motives in my heart. I want to have a pure heart that seeks You for who You are, not just for what You can do for me. Let my desire for spiritual gifts flow from love for You and compassion for others, not pride or performance. Help me distinguish between authentic and artificial spirituality. Give me discernment to recognize the real from the counterfeit. Let my spiritual experiences be rooted in biblical truth and characterized by the fruit of the Spirit. I want to be like the Bereans who were eager to receive Your Word but committed to testing everything against Scripture. Let sincerity be the foundation of every supernatural experience in my life. In Jesus' name, Amen.

PRAYER 3: TOTAL GIFT PACKAGE

UNDERSTANDING ALL THAT IS IN YOU NOW

Holy Spirit, I thank You that when I was born again, You deposited the complete supernatural toolkit in my life. I believe I have received the total gift package of every spiritual gift, every divine ability, and every kingdom resource I need to live a life that brings God glory. Open the eyes of my heart to understand what You've actually placed in me. Help me move from "I need more" to "I need activation." Show me the differences between gifts, ministries, activities, and manifestations so I can steward each dimension appropriately. I reject the lie that spiritual gifts are only for special people or that I have to earn what You've freely given. I embrace the truth that You give gifts as You will, for the common good, and that You've chosen to include me in Your supernatural purposes. Activate what's dormant. Stir up what's been sleeping. Let the seed of Your power that You've planted in me begin to sprout and grow. I eagerly desire spiritual gifts, especially that I may prophesy. In Jesus' name, Amen.

PRAYER 4: UNDER THE INFLUENCE

LIVING IN THE SPIRIT-ACTIVATED LIFE

Holy Spirit, teach me to drink of You. I seek Your fullness, and I invite You to be my daily operating system, not just my emergency contact. I want to live under Your influence every moment of every day. Teach me what it means to be filled with the Spirit as a continuous lifestyle, not just a one-time experience. Show me the difference between being Spirit-filled and Spirit-activated. Help me move beyond just having Your presence to being led by Your power. Let Your influence shape my thoughts, emotions, decisions, and responses to every situation. I surrender control of my life to You. Lead me on the path of righteousness. When I'm tempted to operate in my own wisdom or strength, remind me to depend on Your supernatural guidance and empowerment. Let me be so saturated with Your presence that others encounter something of God when they encounter me. Make me a carrier of Your glory wherever I go. In Jesus' name, Amen.

PRAYER 5: WHAT'S IN THE SOIL?

DEVELOPING THE DISCERNING OF SPIRITUAL THINGS

Lord, I need supernatural sensitivity to distinguish what's from You, what's from my own soul, and what's from the enemy. Give me the gift of discerning of spirits so I can navigate spiritual realities with wisdom and accuracy. Teach me to recognize Your voice above all the other voices that compete for my attention. Help me distinguish between my own thoughts and Your divine thoughts. Show me the difference between soulish emotion and spiritual unction. Protect me from deception while keeping my heart open to genuine spiritual encounters. Teach me to be both wise and innocent in how I approach supernatural experiences. Develop in me the spiritual maturity to test all things and hold fast to what is good. Let discernment be not just a gift I operate in but also a character quality that permeates every area of my life. In Jesus' name, Amen.

PRAYER 6: TONGUES

ACTIVATING PRAYER IN THE SPIRIT

Father, I thank You for the gift of tongues, and I repent of anything that quenches a desire for everything You have for me. You have given tongues as a gift for awakening my spirit and for communication with You. I ask You to lead me in this gift. I lay aside my limited understanding, and I reject any fear, embarrassment, or theological confusion about this gift. I believe what Scripture teaches about speaking in tongues as a gift for personal edification. Let this gift be a gateway to accessing all You have for me. When I pray in the Spirit, let it strengthen my inner man, build my faith, and increase sensitivity to Your voice in other areas. Use this gift to help me pray Your perfect will when I don't know what words to say. Let my prayer be authentic and powerful, not manufactured or superficial. I want to speak to You in mysteries by the Spirit, knowing that You understand every word even when my mind doesn't. In Jesus' name, Amen.

PRAYER 7: SURGE OF FAITH

ACTIVATING THE TURBO GIFT

Holy Spirit, I confess I've been exhausting myself with effort when You've already opened the door. Forgive me for striving in my own strength when Your power was available. I don't want to minister from psychology or human wisdom. I want to recognize when You are present to act and partner with You in those moments. Teach me to discern the difference between natural boldness and supernatural faith. Help me recognize the markers: supernatural peace instead of nervous energy, clarity instead of confusion, focus on Your glory instead of my performance. I ask for the gift of faith to activate everything else You've planted in me. Make me sensitive to ordinary moments when You want to do extraordinary things. Cultivate the soil of my heart through prayer, Scripture, and surrender so that when the surge comes, I'm ready for breakthrough. Make me willing to recognize it and step through the open door. In Jesus' name, Amen.

PRAYER 8: WHEN GOD SPEAKS

ACTIVATING THE INSIGHT GIFTS

Lord, I want to be Your mouthpiece to encourage, edify, and exhort others through prophetic ministry. Give me words that carry Your heart, Your hope, and Your healing to people who need to hear from heaven. Help me distinguish between my own thoughts and Your divine messages. Teach me to speak what I see and hear in the Spirit, even when it doesn't make sense to my natural mind. Let me be faithful to deliver Your words with accuracy and love. Give me courage to step out in prophetic ministry, even when I'm afraid of missing it. Help me learn from my mistakes without becoming paralyzed by the fear of imperfection. Let me grow in prophetic maturity through practice and community correction. Use my voice to call forth destiny in others, to expose enemy lies, and to release Your plans and purposes over people's lives. Let every prophetic word I speak build up the body of Christ and bring glory to Your name. In Jesus' name, Amen.

PRAYER 9: WHEN GOD WORKS

ACTIVATING THE IMPACT GIFTS

Jehovah Rapha, the God who heals, I believe You still work healings and miracles through ordinary believers like me. I ask for the gifts of healings and the working of miracles to flow through my life for Your glory and others' good. Help me approach healing ministry with both faith and compassion, understanding that these gifts reveal Your heart more than they demonstrate my spiritual maturity. Let me minister from relationship with You, not from technique or formula. Give me supernatural faith to pray for the impossible while trusting Your wisdom about timing and methods. Help me handle both dramatic healings and apparent non-responses with equal grace and continued faith. Let me be a conduit of Your resurrection power, bringing healing to the broken, hope to the hopeless, and life to the dead. Use me to demonstrate that Your kingdom is near and Your love is real. In Jesus' name, Amen.

PRAYER 10: THE FAITHFUL STEWARD

LIVING THE SUPERBLOOM

Father, I thank You for everything You've sown in the soil of my life: the Word, the Spirit, the gifts, the calling, the training, and even the struggles that have prepared me for this season. Help me be a faithful steward of all You've entrusted to me. Give me wisdom to cultivate what's growing in my life with patience, intentionality, and holy boldness. Help me resist the pressure to rush Your timing or skip steps in the process of spiritual development. Most importantly, let me remember that the superbloom isn't ulti-

mately about what comes out of the ground of my life but about staying connected to You, the One who owns it all. Let my relationship with You be the foundation of every spiritual experience and the goal of every supernatural encounter. Use me to sow seeds of life, hope, and supernatural possibility in everyone around me. Let my gifts serve others, my resources advance Your kingdom, and my life create hunger for more of You in the people I encounter. Whether You produce a small wildflower or a vast field through my life, let me be faithful in stewarding whatever You choose to bloom. The seeds are Yours, the harvest is Yours, and so am I. In Jesus' name, Amen.

SUPERBLOOM

Group Leader's Guide

Download the *Group Leader's Guide* to assist you in facilitating a small group study of *Superbloom*.

Access it for free at myanchorcollective.com.